Course Design
for
University
Lecturers

Course Design
for
University
Lecturers

Allen H Miller

Kogan Page, London
Nichols Publishing Company, New York

First published in Great Britain in 1987
by Kogan Page Ltd, 120 Pentonville Road,
London N1 9JN

British Library Cataloguing in Publication Data
Miller, Allen H
Course design for university lecturers.
1. Universities and colleges —Curricula
2. Curriculum planning
I. Title
378'.199   LB2361
ISBN 1-85091-277-7

First published in the United States of America in 1987 by
Nichols Publishing Company, Post Office Box 96, New York, NY 10024

Library of Congress Cataloging in Publication Data
Miller, Allen H. (Allen Horace)
Course design for university lecturers.
Bibliography: p.
1. Education, Higher — Great Britain — Curricula.
2. Curriculum planning — Great Britain. 3. Curriculum
evaluation. I. Title.
LB2362.G7M54 1987   373'.199'0941   86-28629
ISBN 0-89397-268-1

Printed in Great Britain by
Dotesios (Printers) Limited
Bradford-on-Avon, Wiltshire

Table of Contents

PREFACE

The design of a university or college course is, in some institutions, left entirely to the person who will be teaching that course, whereas in other institutions the teacher will be assisted by a Division of Educational Technology. *Course Design for University Lecturers* has been written to help the former group of college and university teachers who are unable to seek the advice of others with a specialised knowledge of the principles of curriculum theory or educational psychology. Despite its title, the book does attempt to address the needs of teachers in all types of tertiary institutions. While a majority of examples have been drawn from universities, chiefly in the United Kingdom and Australia, reference is also made to courses in Colleges of Advaned Education, Colleges of Technical and Further Education and the needs of teachers in these institutions.

In this book I have drawn on my own experiences, first as a college and university lecturer and then as a consultant to university teachers, and on the research findings of others, as reported in the literature on Higher Education. I am very grateful to those who have given me permission to quote from their earlier work on this subject and to colleagues in Australia, Scotland, England, Sweden, Germany, Canada, the United States and Thailand who were very generous with their time in describing their work.

The opening chapter includes definitions of terms used throughout the book which have different meanings in different English-speaking countries. In the second chapter the importance of clarifying what one is trying to do in a university or college course is considered. This is followed by a chapter which draws attention to the effect of differing backgrounds on students' performance. The fourth and fifth chapters deal with the central issues of course planning, with an emphasis on the selection of content and teaching methods which are most appropriate for achieving the aims of a course.

The effectiveness of a course plan becomes known when students have been assessed and their attitudes to the course evaluated. These matters are treated in the last two chapters which are relatively long ones, the length being indicative of the importance of assessment and evaluation in any course planning exercise. Throughout the book detailed references are given to more extensive literature on the subjects being discussed. One of the functions of *Course Design for University Lecturers* is to provide a guide to such literature.

The book would not have been possible without the cooperation of The Australian National University (ANU) which, through its Outside Studies Programs, has allowed me to examine at first hand the work being done to improve teaching and learning in other universities and colleges. My colleagues in the Office for Research in Academic Methods (ORAM) within the ANU have also contributed indirectly to this book as many of the procedures described, particularly those with regard to the evaluation of courses, have been developed through the joint efforts of all members of ORAM staff. Throughout the long gestation period for this book my wife was a source of encouragement and a help in avoiding an over-use of technical jargon.

The publication is an interesting application of the new technologies available to academics, in that I made extensive use of the text processing facilities on mainframe and micro computers during all stages of preparation. These facilities were particularly helpful in keeping a track of references and when preparing the index.

The book was planned and partly written while I was a Visiting Fellow in the Institute for Research and Development into Post-Compulsory Education at the University of Lancaster in 1983. I typed the text into Lancaster's newly installed VAX computer, copied the material to tape for bringing back to Australia, transferred the draft chapters first to a DEC-10 in the ANU and then, when VAX computers became available in the ANU, to the computer on which I completed the writing.

As the book was developed the revision of drafts was facilitated by transferring some text from the VAX to my personal Apple Macintosh microcomputer, editing the text on the more accessible Macintosh and transferring it back to the VAX. The final stages of text processing, preparation of a bibliography and index, and printing a master copy was completed on an ANU VAX.

Allen H. Miller   Office for Research in Academic Methods

November 1986   Australian National University, Canberra

1. WHAT THIS BOOK IS ABOUT

1.1. ACADEMICS AND COURSE DESIGN

University and college teachers are usually well qualified in their particular subject field or discipline and are expected to have special expertise in at least one particular field of study. When faced with the responsibility of developing a new course or teaching program, however, most have little, if any, background in the educational theories of teaching and learning, and many have problems in deciding which subject matter to include in the new course.

Robert Gagné, whose writings about education have been an inspiration to many classroom teachers, describes the situation of the university or college teacher and illustrates the need for taking into consideration the theoretical basis of course design in the following passage:

> Instruction of college and university students is an activity not customarily derived in a deliberate fashion from theories about learning. Most college instructors set about their initial task of teaching courses by using a model derived from their own college experiences; in other words, they try to emulate their own professors. The new instructor may spend many hours in selecting a text and other references, in planning what he will say to his class of students, in seeing how certain topics will "fit" a semester of so many weeks. But the question of just what the students are going to be doing during these weeks, and how their activities are going to affect their capabilities, is not likely to be given a great deal of thought. (Gagné, 1971, p. 299)

This book is intended as a guide to university and college teachers who have had no formal training in education. Some basic principles of the theories of effective teaching and learning are presented in a logical sequence and these are illustrated with examples from university and college courses in a number of countries. No prior knowledge of educational terminology is assumed, although some technical terms will be introduced at appropriate stages. The book does not attempt to replace formal courses in curriculum design in higher education which can provide a much more thorough approach to the topic than is possible in a relatively small volume. Nevertheless one would hope that it will be found suitable for adoption as a text in programs leading to formal qualifications in tertiary teaching.

In order to restrict the length to manageable proportions for those wishing to use this as a handbook, some topics receive fairly superficial treatment, but in such cases reference is made to a selection of literature where the subject is dealt with in greater depth.

The set of questions on the back cover is designed to provide a framework for the course developer, but they could also be used as a checklist for university and college teachers wishing to evaluate their own programs. Thus those who are already teaching courses would find it helpful to read carefully through these questions before moving on to the next chapter, answering those questions which are applicable to their courses. Throughout the book reference will be made to these and similar questions, as readers are guided to answers which are most appropriate for their courses and institutions. The questions are repeated in the final chapter in order to provide a useful set of reminders for revision purposes when preparing new or revised teaching programs.

It is unfortunate that in Education, as in some other disciplines, words have been given alternative meanings by different groups of people. In the remainder of this chapter the terms which are used repeatedly throughout the book are defined in order to avoid any confusion.

1.2. LEVELS OF EDUCATION

Primary education as used in this book refers to that section of full-time schooling which usually begins when a child is between five and seven and extends for six or seven years. In some countries, this may be the only form of education for the majority of the population, but whenever students are likely to proceed to a university or college education, primary schooling will be followed by secondary. The main distinction between primary and secondary education is the transition from class or grade teaching to subject teaching. In the United States, the word "primary" is applied to the first year or two of "elementary" education, with the word "elementary" being used in the sense described for "primary" above.

Secondary education varies in form from one part of the world to another. In some regions more than one form of secondary education exists so that pupils, or their parents, have a choice. Some educational authorities have found it advantageous to organise their secondary schools at two levels, with the upper level tending to concentrate more on preparation for studies in higher education.

Tertiary education is a term that has differing connotations in various places. For the purpose of this book I shall use the term to describe all education which occurs after secondary education, whether the students have completed the formal requirements of secondary education or not. Thus it includes technical, further and higher education.

1.3. THE CURRICULUM IN HIGHER EDUCATION

The word "curriculum" is widely used in connection with school learning experiences, but is less common in relation to higher education. Eraut (1975) describes "curriculum" as:

> the set of broad inter-related decisions about what is taught that characterise the general framework within which teaching is planned and learning takes place.

In the context of higher education a good working definition would be "the total planned learning program for any one student". There are good reasons why curricula at the tertiary level should be defined in terms of the planned learning experiences for individual students. Even though fairly large numbers of students may be enrolled in a common pattern of courses which make up the total curriculum for the award of a degree. it is normal for students to be given some choice in subjects, particularly in their later years and considerable choice of essay or assignment topics within even the compulsory courses.

By way of contrast, in primary schools it is common for the total curriculum to be planned, at least for each school class, so that all children in the one class follow essentially the same program of studies. Streaming and selection of optional subjects are both common in secondary curricula, but in many countries, there is still a substantial core curriculum followed by all students. At the tertiary level students who are undertaking professional studies such as Electrical Engineering, Dentistry, or Law, or trade courses such as Plumbing or Hairdressing may follow a curriculum which is virtually the same for all students in the faculty, whereas in Arts, Science and Economics each student in effect constructs a curriculum from the smorgasborg of courses which best suits his or her own needs and interests.

Thus the main influence an institution can have on the curriculum is through regulations governing the sequencing of units and an insistence that students must study some subjects "in depth" for two or, more usually, three years.

1.3.1. Courses and Units

The word "course" is used more loosely than most of the other terms being defined in this section. It is sometimes confused with curriculum, such as when a student says, "I am enrolling for the course in Business Administration", when he/she is about to commence an M.B.A. degree. More frequently the word refers to individual units of study taken over a limited period of a year or a semester, such as Statistics A01 or Plant Anatomy. "Unit" tends to be used interchangeably with "course"; in this book I shall use the word "course" to describe a relatively self-contained sequence of studies for which a student enrols and which is eventually examined. While a single course may contain optional components, it is treated as an entity for administrative purposes.

1.3.2. Subjects or Disciplines?

In this book I shall use the terms "subject" or "discipline" more or less interchangeably to refer to clearly identifiable areas of knowledge which may be studied independently from or together with other such areas of knowledge. It is unfortunate that "subject" is sometimes applied equally to what is taught in a traditional university department, such as Botany, and subdivisions of that "subject", such as Plant Morphology or Mycology. When I wish to distinguish between the two levels I shall use the word "discipline" to apply to the wider field of study and "subject" for the narrower.

1.3.3. Syllabus

The term "syllabus" is used more commonly with reference to primary or secondary education, but may equally well be applied at the tertiary levels. It refers to any written outline of subject matter which the teacher plans to cover in a course. Sometimes the syllabus is prescribed by a government authority, but at the university level in particular it is more frequently prepared by the teacher.

1.3.4. Modules

"Module" is a term which has been introduced into educational literature in recent years and is usually more clearly defined than "course" or "unit". The Group for Research and Innovation in Higher Education (1976) states that in British usage "module" is the preferred term for use in polytechnics and "unit" in universities, but elsewhere "modular instruction" is the process of breaking up a curriculum (or course) into relatively small areas of study, each of which may last from a few weeks to a whole semester. The advantages and disadvantages of breaking a single course into a number of modules, from which a student selects a predetermined number for study, will be discussed in more detail later. At this stage it is sufficient to say that modularisation allows a teacher to plan in some detail the content and methods of presentation while retaining a degree of flexibility for different types of student needs.

1.3.5. Programs

As with some of the other terms, the word "program" is used in a number of different educational contexts. Its use in connection with computing is well known and later I shall make reference to some programs which are useful in designing Computer Assisted Instruction. In those primary and secondary schools where teachers are under a fairly high level of supervision the word applies to a detailed summary of the teacher's day-to-day activities, supposedly compiled for the teacher's benefit, but generally required as a demonstration to the supervisor that the teacher is conscientious. At the tertiary level the word is also sometimes used as a synonym for "course" or "unit", but in one university at least the word is used to distinguish between what is taught in a Department, which usually deals with the one discipline, and that which is taught by an inter-disciplinary team. Two examples from the Australian National University are Women's Studies and Human Sciences.

1.3.6. Majors and Minors

A "major" is a sequence of courses or units in the one subject taken by a student in order to provide depth to the degree program, usually over a period of three or more years. A "minor" is a shorter sequence, usually two years.

1.3.7. Teachers

In this book I shall normally refer to those who have teaching responsibilities in a university or college by the generic term of "teachers". The term thus includes teaching assistants, instructors, tutors, lecturers, professors and various levels among these posts.

1.4. COMPLEXITIES OF COURSE DESIGN

The task of course design is far more than the preparation of a document which outlines the content to be taught, lists essential and recommended readings and sets essay topics. The designer also needs to consider the context in which the course will be offered, effective methods for developing the necessary knowledge, skills and attitudes in students, resources required, measures of student learning and a plan for evaluating the course at regular intervals. In the chapters which follow each of these matters will be considered.

2. WHY IS THIS COURSE BEING TAUGHT?

A course may be designed to help prepare students for a profession or trade or to cater for specific needs or interests of selected students. Its main justification, on the other hand, may simply be to provide intellectual stimulation or sheer enjoyment. The content of the course may be decided mainly by the teacher, by its students after they enrol, or it could be dictated by a higher authority, such as a university faculty, a professional body or a government authority.

With all of these possibilities, it is important that those preparing to teach a course should consider the question which forms the title of this chapter and which also heads the list of questions inside the front cover. Even when the content of the course is fairly tightly prescribed by an outside authority, the teacher has some degree of freedom in the manner of presentation. In deciding which topics are to be given greater emphasis a teacher indicates either directly or indirectly that some topics are more important than others. It is possible, for example, for a teacher to *say* that students are encouraged to demonstrate original thought, but *expect* the students to reproduce in examinations the exact lines of reasoning used by the teacher.

2.1. OBJECTIVES FOR A TOTAL CURRICULUM

It would be rare to find a college or university which prescribes its curriculum in detail for a general degree program such as Arts or Science. A prescriptive pattern of studies is, however, much more common in professional degrees, such as Engineering, Law and Medicine. Whether the patterns of courses leading to a degree are prescribed or not it is important for academic staff to give some attention to what it is they hope their students will achieve as a result of their tertiary studies.

Examples can be found among courses leading to professional qualifications where there have been marked changes from the traditional approach in direct response to the projected needs of the profession. A relatively recent example comes from the Faculty of Medicine in the University of Newcastle, New South Wales. The Foundation Dean, the late Professor David Maddison, had been dean of a medical faculty in another university where a pattern of courses leading to a highly valued degree had been evolved over a very long period of time. When given the opportunity to establish a new faculty and curriculum, Maddison and his faculty sought to identify the characteristics which might be expected in a medical graduate in the nineteen-eighties and beyond.

At a very early stage in the development of the Newcastle curriculum, the Faculty listed a series of objectives for the total program. They related these to six areas of learning, only one of which corresponds in any way to the major divisions of a "traditional" medical curriculum. In fact many of the objectives could be adopted, either directly or with one or two words changed, in other professional programs. For this reason they are well worth examining in some detail. A few representative examples of objectives for each of the six main areas of the Newcastle medical curriculum are given below:

The Faculty of Medicine at the University of Newcastle proposes to develop an educational programme designed to ensure that, at its conclusion, the graduate:

1. [The Student's Own Learning]

   a. has demonstrated his ability to locate biomedical information required for the understanding and management of medical problems, through an appropriate use of available educational resources;

   b. has demonstrated the ability to monitor, granted appropriate consultation, his own progress in the acquisition of information and skills;

2. [Scientific Method and Procedure]

   a. has demonstrated that he can make reliable observations of cellular, physiological and behavioural phenomena, and that he can extract the relevant data from these observations, integrating where appropriate the information provided from these three perspectives on human biology;

   b. has demonstrated his ability to assess the reliability of conclusions based on reported data, and to comprehend the standard forms of statistical treatment employed for the analysis of such data;

3. [Clinical Diagnosis, Investigation and Management]

   a. has demonstrated his understanding of the mechanism and significance of health-related physical and behavioural events, normal and abnormal, at levels ranging from molecular to that of the community and the wider environment;

   b. has demonstrated the ability and willingness to apply his understanding of biological mechanisms to the diagnosis and management of illness;

   c. has demonstrated the ability and willingness to apply his understanding of psychological and social mechanisms to the diagnosis and management of illness;

   d. has demonstrated his ability and willingness to devise and maintain an approriate management programme for patients with chronic, intractable illness, including terminal disease;

4. [Attitudes and Personal Characteristics]

   a. manifests those personal characteristics essential for the effective practice of medicine, including

      i. an awareness of his own assets, limitations and responsiveness,

      ii. responsibility, thoroughness, trustworthiness and confidentiality,

      iii. sensitivity to the needs of others and concern for other persons;

   b. has demonstrated that his approach to all patients reflects the attitude that the person who is ill is more important than the illness from which he suffers;

5. [Community Medicine]

   a. has demonstrated his understanding of the importance of environmental factors in the causation and maintenance of illness, and in its response to treatment;

   b. has demonstrated a positive, consistent and informed attitude towards the prevention of illness and the maintenance of health, at both individual and population levels;

   c. manifests a positive attitude towards the concept of the physician as an educator, for example to his patients with regard to their illnesses, to the public in matters of health and to his colleagues in professional matters and relationships, and shows an appropriate level of ability and confidence in this role;

6. [Doctor/Patient Relationship]

   a. has demonstrated an awareness of how his own personality affects his interactions with his patients and how his own anxiety and prejudices may alter patient attitudes and behaviour.

(Engel and Clarke, 1979, p. 71)

Having identified the objectives for the total curriculum, the Newcastle faculty then adopted a system of teaching and learning which would enable their students to progress towards the attainment of these objectives. The curriculum which the Newcastle team developed, and which is now being evaluated by monitoring the careers of its first graduates, placed considerable emphasis on the solution of problems likely to be encountered in general practice. These problems were investigated by groups of students working under the guidance of faculty tutors, with each group being able to call upon the resources of the faculty or of nearby hospitals (Engel and Clarke, 1979).

Despite the marked changes in organisation of subject matter and methods of teaching. this curriculum aimed to produce graduates who could work with graduates from other universities and who would not be disadvantaged by the "Newcastle experiment" (Engel. Clarke and Feletti, 1982). Newcastle graduates would be expected to have a similar range of knowledge and skills to graduates from more traditional faculties. Whether the "experiment" has been successful or not will only be known when the first graduates have had some years of experience in their profession.

Attempts by the University of Newcastle to take into account the changing needs of the community and of present day medical practitioners are not unique. The University of Aston in Birmingham offers a program leading to the award of a B.Sc. in Building in which the needs of the community influence the direction taken by the total curriculum. A prospectus issued in 1977 has the following to say about the importance of the building industry and the function of their degree program:

Building is concerned with satisfying the needs of people. The majority of human activities cannot be carried out without a building or covered structure of some kind. It follows that the construction industry, probably more than any other, has the opportunity, and the responsibility of making knowledge work for the benefit of the community.

It is the second largest industry in Britain and accounts for about half of the country's capital expenditure. To those who seek variety in their career, it offers active participation in endeavours to improve the quality of the environment through the application of new materials and techniques, the ability to utilise organizational and managerial skills, and to be involved in financial and economic decisions. (Aston, 1977, p. 51)

In a similar manner the University of Stirling indicates how the study of history might contribute to one's university education:

The teaching of history at Stirling aims to provide an appropriate education, not only for students who wish to become professional historians, but also for those who wish to combine a general intellectual training with the acquisition of a background to the understanding of the contemporary world. (Stirling, 1983, p. 80)

2.2. THE PLACE OF OBJECTIVES IN PLANNING SINGLE COURSES

In the last few paragraphs I have focussed on a total curriculum, but for many university or college teachers, the task is the preparation of a single course. For those responsible for first year courses, there are special responsibilities to all other members of the department or faculty and a decision has to be made as to whether the course should attempt to survey the discipline or provide a firm basis for later studies or both (Miller, 1980).

2.2.1. What do we Mean by Objectives?

There is a certain amount of confusion in educational literature about words such as "purpose", "aim", "goal", and "objective". In this section I shall try to clarify the meaning of these words, at least in terms of current educational usage. It is probably less confusing to start with **objectives**, which have been defined by Blishen (1969) as:

(Objectives) tell the pupil what the minimum level of acceptance for his or her eventual performance is to be, and under what conditions it will be achieved. To be meaningful, any statement of objectives must specify observable, preferably measurable, changes in the learner's behaviour at the end of the course.

It will be seen from the above description and similar ones by Tyler (1950) and Mager (1962) that the emphasis is on observable behaviours in students which might be used as evidence that the course is being successfully taught and learned. It will be noted that in the above description, the word "changes" implies that the behaviours which illustrate mastery of knowledge or skills will have been learned in the course; one can envisage a situation when students would have been able to demonstrate them before enrolling. Mager (1962) also claims that clearly defined objectives will state what a student must be able to do at certain stages in a course and they must specify the conditions under which the activities are likely to occur. Unlike Blishen, Mager claims that a statement of objectives should also indicate the level of competency which is to be demonstrated. Beard, Healey and Holloway (1974, pp. 77-78) illustrate the specificity of objectives sought by Mager in the following example from part of one course in a medical curriculum:

Under hospital ward conditions, the resident house officer will be able to demonstrate that he can:-

1. diagnose cardiac arrests;

2. initiate and carry out cardiac massage and artificial ventilation;

3. initiate and assist at

    a. improving ventilation;

    b. ECG interpretation;

    c. drug therapy;

    d. defibrilation;

4. decide when resuscitation measures ought not to have been instituted;

5. assess when cardiac massage can cease.

Even more specific objectives are stated for Newcastle students when confronted by a patient who describes certain symptoms, such as abdominal pain (Engel and Clarke, 1979, p. 72). By stating the objectives with such specificity it is possible for students and their tutors to check more easily whether each student has the knowledge and skills expected. Admittedly it is more difficult to check whether objectives relating to the development of attitudes have been achieved.

One other example of a set of objectives, this time in the physical sciences, is given by Dawes (1972, p. 205) for a chemistry course in which the aim includes a reference to "the significance of scientific processes". Dawes suggests that relevant objectives might be:

Students should be able to present and discuss, orally or in written form, arguments related to

1. the influence of natural resources on the living standards and wealth of a country, e.g. opal, oil, natural gas, iron, nickel, copper:

2. the need for wise use of natural resources;

3. the conflict in choice between conservation and exploitation of resources:

4. the importance of scientific processes in agriculture, commerce and industry.

Critics of the above statements as behavioural objectives would point out that the statements do not specify the level of performance expected of students. They would also be justified in claiming that more than one answer would be acceptable in answer to the questions implied by the objectives.

2.3. AIMS AND GOALS

Whereas an objective specifies things which a student will be able to do at certain points in a course, an **aim** describes the intended direction of the course. As Davies (1976, p. 12) says:

> Aims are a starting point. They are an ideal, an aspiration a direction in which to go. They are visionary in character, and therefore, in a very real sense, unreal.

Sometimes statements of aims are incorporated into official documents outlining a curriculum or a particular course of study. The following example from the University of Stirling's Prospectus indicates the aims for their courses in Education and gives some indication of how these aims will be achieved. It should be noted, however, that the statement does not attempt to specify objectives:

> Education courses at Stirling aim to provide students with the knowledge and experience necessary to the understanding of the processes of teaching and learning and to develop thoughtful and effective ways of teaching. Emphasis is placed upon the integration of theoretical and practical work, opportunities for individualised study, close contacts between tutors and students and the use of video feedback for studying one's own teaching.

Two further examples, this time from the Australian National University, illustrate broad aims each of which could be applied to more than one course.

> To give the student an understanding of the economic system and to analyse the central problems of government economic policy.

> To give some insight into the objective and scientific study of human behaviour.

It will be noted that each of the above aims is very general and neither of them attempts to say how they will be achieved. That is not the function of aims. It is the task of the course planner to translate general aims such as these into objectives, but it should be noted that any attempt to list objectives without a consideration of the broader aims can lead to undue emphasis being given to trivial attainments or ones which have no direct reference to the aims.

As an attempt to bridge the gap between **aims**, which are broad statements of intent, and **objectives**, which are specifications of behaviour expected of students at the end of a course or at key points in it, some educationists have used the word **goals**. It may be helpful to use metaphors developed by Davies (1976) who pictures an aim as a starting point and direction, objectives as a series of signposts or milestones of achievement and the goal as the final destination. In another section of his book, Davies likens aims to ends and goals to the means by which the ends are achieved.

2.4. WHY SPECIFY OBJECTIVES?

Before leaving this section devoted to aims, goals and objectives, it is important to consider briefly some of the arguments about the usefulness or otherwise of specifying objectives in higher education. Readers who wish to pursue this issue in greater depth are urged to consult one of the publications devoted to the topic, such as Beard, Healey and Holloway (1974), Bloom, Hastings and Madaus (1971), Davies (1976) and appropriate chapters in Hooper (1983) or Rowntree (1974). For a more critical evaluation of the use of objectives in the planning of university courses, the well reasoned article by MacDonald-Ross (1973) should be consulted.

Some important benefits which Rowntree (1974, pp. 35-36) attributes to the practice of clearly formulating one's objectives in behavioural terms may be summarised as follows:

1. (Behavioural objectives) make it possible for teachers to communicate their intentions more clearly to colleagues and students.

2. They provide a framework for the selection of course content and structure.

3. They guide in the selection of appropriate teaching and learning methods.

4. They help the teacher decide what are the most appropriate means for evaluation and assessment.

2.4.1. Stating Objectives Clearly

Rowntree (1974, p. 58) lists a number of words which should be avoided and a similar number which should be used when a person is trying to state objectives as unambigously as possible. A selection from Rowntree's list is given in Table 2.1 below.

AVOID words like:	USE words like:
Know	List
Understand	Describe
Be familiar with	Evaluate
Become acqainted with	State
Have a good grasp of	Explain
Obtain a working knowledge of	Select
Appreciate	Identify
Realise the significance of	Distinguish
Be aware of	Design
Believe	Construct
Be interested in	Solve

Although the above list is arranged in pairs of contrasting words or phrases there is no suggestion that the word in the second column is meant to replace the word or phrase in the same row of the first column. It should also be understood that in proscribing certain words like "know". "understand", "appreciate" and "interest", Rowntree is not suggesting that these are not worth-while goals for a university or college student. He is saying, however, that these words are inappropriate for describing how a teacher will recognise whether goals seeking knowledge, appreciation or understanding have been achieved.

2.5. OBJECTIONS TO OBJECTIVES

By way of contrast, to the above, MacDonald-Ross (1973) claims that there are fundamental weaknesses in an educational technology which places too much importance on objectives. He says that those who advocate the use of behavioural objectives in curriculum planning overlook or avoid the important issue of how these objectives are chosen. Important questions of value are not discussed, yet it is a combination of social and individual values, he claims, which lead a teacher to a particular form of presentation or students to their own directions in learning. Moreover a list of a large number of behavioural objectives can in no way express the logical structure of the subject or the relationships between topics.

MacDonald-Ross also states that decisions about what is to be taught must precede any formulation of goals or behavioural objectives. He points out that even when objectives have been stated clearly, students will make choices about what should be learned by them, regardless of what the teacher expects. While one cannot object to his last statement, there are many who would raise strong objections to the first. The majority of writers on curriculum theory state that the formulation of aims and objectives must at least occur concurrently with the selection of content, and in many courses the formulation of aims and objectives will occur first.

Another weakness, according to MacDonald-Ross, can be traced to the origin of the behavioural objectives movement which was associated with the writing of programmed instruction for teaching the manipulative skills needed for operating equipment in the American armed forces. Behavioural objectives were developed as a result of watching the activities of a "master performer" operate the equipment, deciding the best sequence for learning each operation, and writing a program to teach the operations in the correct sequence. MacDonald-Ross identifies a number of flaws in the above approach to the specification of objectives in academic studies. In the first instance there is the difficulty of identifying a master performer and, secondly, it is impossible to guarantee that the skills shown by one master performer will be the same as those shown by another. A third problem with defining behavioral objectives in terms of skills or knowledge demonstrated by a master performer is that when a new course is being taught, particularly in an emerging discipline or a multi-disciplinary field, it is likely that no master performers are available to demonstrate the desired behaviours (*ibid*).

2.6. WHY USE OBJECTIVES?

It should be clear from the earlier sections of this chapter that there are fairly substantial arguments for and against the use of behavioural objectives in higher education. Many of those who omit any mention of objectives in their course outlines do so, not so much because they are opposed to the principle, but because they lack the time needed to formulate objectives for a course or they do not know how to write objectives. On the other hand, there are lecturers who report that the discipline of thinking about objectives helps them to plan more efficiently for students' learning experiences and for assessment tasks.

There is always a danger that an over-emphasis on behavioural objectives will result in a failure to work towards the more intangible aims of a course which are typified by words or phrases such as those in the first column of Rowntree's list which was reproduced earlier in this chapter. The conscientious course planner will experiment with varying degrees of specificity until the most effective balance is found between broader expectations and narrower statements of how a student will demonstrate successful learning in a program of study.

MacDonald-Ross has rightly highlighted the dangers of poorly formulated objectives but, on balance, there are strong arguments for specifying what students should be able to do to demonstrate what they have learned during a course and the conditions under which they should be able to demonstrate this learning. When discussing assessment in Chapter 6 I will be referring to the relationship between levels of objectives and types of assessment.

3. STUDENT BACKGROUNDS AND LEARNING

One of the side effects of the rapid expansion of all forms of tertiary education in the 1960s and early 1970s has been the considerable extension of the range of abilities and backgrounds among tertiary students. With rapidly changing employment opportunities, students' reasons for attending college or university are often ill-defined, and this may affect their attitude to study. In Australia, for example, the composition of the student population has changed as more mature-age students return to study and more students come from homes where the parents, or the students themselves, were not born in an English-speaking country. These changes are more apparent in universities than in colleges, where there has always been a fairly high proportion of older students.

By 1983 another change in the composition of the student population could be discerned in Australia, namely a decrease in the number of school leavers entering higher education, possibly as a result of the difficult economic climate from 1980 to 1982. Comparable changes can be identified among student populations in other countries.

With so many changes in the background, age and motivation of first year students in higher education it is important that their teachers should understand how differences among students might influence learning. Wherever possible course designers should make provision for these differences in the design of courses.

Sometimes a teacher will have little control over the selection of content, as this is decided by a government authority or the faculty in which the course is taught. It is nevertheless still possible to make some provision for differences among students. The first and perhaps the bluntest approach is to restrict the entrance of unsuitable students to the course by refusing to enrol those deemed to have insufficient qualifications. Alternatively, one could attempt to discourage those who are likely to be unsuitable by means of a statement about pre-requisites or levels of assumed knowledge in the faculty handbook or course guide.

3.1. PRE-REQUISITES

The specification of a required level of entry to a course is by far the most common method of restricting the course to students who have the requisite background knowledge and skills. For advanced level courses it is normal to require that entering students will have completed certain lower level courses, either in the same subject or in a closely related one. Sometimes students are expected to have also completed a service course, such as statistics before undertaking higher level courses in a social science.

Many first year courses specify that entering students must have taken similar subjects at particular levels at secondary school. In countries where there is considerable variation between what is taught in similarly named subjects at the secondary and tertiary levels, or where the tertiary institution is admitting students from many different school systems or countries, it is important that the statement about pre-requisites specify the type of knowledge or skills required in entering students. If there is some doubt about levels of students from different school systems, a diagnostic test may be used to identify those students who will or will not be admitted to the course. The test results will also pinpoint for the teacher which areas of subject matter are likely to prove difficult for some students.

There are occasions when a teacher is prepared to enrol a wider range of students than would normally be admitted if the rules about pre-requisites were strictly applied. Under these conditions the new students should be informed that the teacher will work on the assumption that students have either reached a satisfactory level in pre-requisite studies or have undertaken extra reading which is usually specified by the teacher. Some academic departments provide bridging courses during the vacation prior to the commencement of an academic year in order to bring students up to a more or less common standard.

3.2. STUDENT CHARACTERISTICS AFFECTING LEARNING

The foregoing discussion relates mainly to students' previous formal studies of the discipline which they wish to study at the tertiary level. Other intellectual factors which should be considered if possible are the degrees of literacy and numeracy of students and their levels of understanding in related subjects such as statistics, chemistry or grammar.

If the students come from a different culture from that of the majority of students and staff, there may also be language or social problems to be overcome. Obviously a university or college teacher does not have the time nor the expertise to deal with all the problems that are likely to arise, consequently the provision by the institution of student services, such as health, counselling, or study centres, is a great advantage.

Among the "non academic" aspects of a student's characteristics which affect learning are the student's habitual approaches to study and attitudes to learning. Much research has been conducted on these attributes of students in recent years and only a selection of the findings can be included here. For a very clear account of the earlier work on student learning, readers should consult the small book by Entwistle and Hounsell (1975) in which many of those who were conducting research at that time have described their findings. A recent survey article by Ramsden (1985) summarises much of the important research in this area to date.

3.2.1. Learning Strategies

Major contributions to our understanding of student learning have been made by researchers in Sweden, the United Kingdom, Australia and other parts of the world, with much of this research being integrated through an informal network of researchers. The research team which has probably done more than any other group to describe students' approaches to learning is that led by Ference Marton in Gothenburg, Sweden. Combining experimental methods with interview techniques advocated by Parlett and Hamilton (1972) for the "illuminative evaluation" of innovatory teaching programs, Marton and his associates interviewed university students from a number of different disciplines, questioning them in detail about the approaches they took in reading a set piece of text or writing an essay.

Marton and Säljö (1976), in describing their earlier work, identify two levels of approach to learning tasks or levels of processing information, namely "deep" and "surface". A deep approach, they claim, is characterised by an intention on the part of the student to seek the author's meaning when reading a passage from a reference, to consider the evidence presented and conclusions drawn by the author in order to reach a personal conclusion, and attempts to relate the new knowledge to the student's previous knowledge or experience in the new world. A surface approach, on the other hand, is used when a student concentrates on memorising discrete facts or ideas, or concentrates on completing a set task. Students who approach their learning tasks in a superficial manner may fail to recognise the hierarchical structure of the text and they are likely to confuse examples with principles. (See also Entwistle, 1982, Säljö, 1982 and Marton, Hounsell & Entwistle, 1984)

At one stage it was thought that students habitually followed one or other of the above approaches to learning and this seemed to be confirmed by parallel research undertaken by Pask (1972) who identified two basic learning strategies which he called "serialist" and "holist". In Pask's earlier papers he described a **serialist** approach as one in which students learn, remember and recapitulate a body of information in a relatively fixed sequence, consequently they find it almost impossible to tolerate irrelevant information unless they are equipped with unusually large memory capacities. A **holist** approach, on the other hand, is one in which students learn, remember and recapitulate as a whole. Students who use the holist strategy are more likely to grasp general principles, Pask claims, than are serialists, but their memory for details is not as accurate (Pask and Scott, 1972).

According to Daniel (1975), who has interpreted some of Pask's work for a wider audience, the existence of the serialist/holist dichotomy is further attested by the evidence that if holists are presented with a teaching program designed for serialists (or vice versa), there is a highly significant decrease in the amount of learning compared with that which occurs when the program is matched to the characteristics of the learner. When students are presented with a learning task designed to allow a choice of either a serialist or holist approach, the two groups perform equally well. Moreover, when each group is asked to teach the newly learned material, they do so following the procedures, serialist or holist, which they themselves have followed.

While it is unrealistic to expect tertiary institutions to allocate students to classes which are appropriate to their learning strategies (assuming that students really do fall into the categories described by Pask), it is not unreasonable to examine carefully all systems of teaching which expect students to follow a rigidly predetermined sequence of learning tasks such as is found in some laboratory courses and audio-tutorials (see Chapter 5).

More recent research by Laurillard (1979), Ramsden (1979), Hounsell (1979) and Säljö (1982) has cast considerable doubt on the stability of the serialist/holist and deep/surface dichotomies. Students have been observed to demonstrate what a number of them call a "versatile" approach to learning tasks, using whichever strategy they think is the most appropriate. Although some students are able to demonstrate versatility, others habitually use learning strategies which are inappropriate for achieving higher level objectives such as the ability to analyse a complex set of data or to integrate new learning with their previous knowledge.

3.2.2. Stages of Intellectual Development

Piaget's theories of mental development in young children have had considerable influence on school courses, particularly in mathematics and the sciences. Evidence cited by Entwistle (1981, pp. 169-173) suggests that some university students may not have reached the level of cognitive development which would enable them to deal with abstract concepts. Diagnostic tests or interviews could be used to identify such students so that teachers can offer assistance and informed advice about their prospects in courses which demand high levels of abstraction.

A rather different interpretation of intellectual and ethical development in college and university students has been proposed by Perry (1970), who claims to have identified nine developmental stages. At the lowest level students rely heavily on authority to tell them what is right and wrong; they therefore seek to discover what are the "facts" and what is the "right" answer to each problem. By the third stage students are able to recognise that certain problems may have more than one legitimate answer and that there is not always a clear distinction between right and wrong, but they attribute this lack of clarity to a failure on the part of the authorities to formulate correct answers at this stage in the advancement of knowledge.

The fourth level, according to Perry, may be summarised by the statement that "Everyone is entitled to his own opinions", in other words the concepts of right and wrong are virtually meaningless. From this fourth level some students may progress through a relativist position to the final stage in which they are developing their own intellectual and ethical commitments within a framework of relativism.

Although Perry has not extended his studies to include stages of intellectual and ethical development of university teachers, one wonders what the effect would be if a teacher is at a lower level of intellectual development than the students: whether the teacher would be expecting "facts" when some of the students do not believe that it is legitimate to seek facts on the issue in question. One of the main criticisms of True-False and Multiple-Choice questions in tests of final achievement is that they tend to operate at Perry's lowest level of "right answers" and do not allow for legitimate differences in interpretation.

It may, of course, be that Perry's stages amount to a valid description of normal maturation which is unrelated to college experience, or simply to the changing attitudes among students generally during the period of his research (the late 1960s). If, however, they really do represent changes due to higher education, it would be consistent with the broader aims of a university for teachers to help their students progress through these stages. Even if Perry's ninth stage is not consistent with the goals of a particular teacher or course, it would be desirable for the teacher to become aware of the stages which have been reached by his/her students.

If an appreciable number of students really do progress through the developmental stages described by Perry, there are clear implications for university and college teachers, particularly when they are planning to use discussions or seminars as part of their teaching program. Cockburn and Ross (1977f. p. 8) demonstrate the links between students' stages of intellectual development and the most suitable type of seminar or discussion class in a table which is reproduced in Chapter 5 of this book.

3.2.3. Orientation to Examinations

Closely related to Perry's stages of development are the techniques used by students in their approaches to study for examinations, according to evidence gathered by Miller and Parlett (1974). After a series of interviews of staff and students in the departments of Law, History and Physics in the University of Edinburgh, they identified three quite distinctive approaches which correspond roughly to the lower, middle and upper levels of Perry's stages. Miller and Parlett describe their three types of students as being "cue-deaf", "cue-conscious" or "cue-seekers", depending on the extent to which the students are aware of cues concerning what is expected of them in a coming exam and the extent to which they actively seek this information.

Cue-seekers appear to be aware of the way the examination system works, they recognise any problems they may still have in knowing how to perform well, and they deliberately set about solving these problems. Miller and Parlett claim that these students, who are also the best performers, are not just "playing the system". They really study hard and are most likely to engage in informal discussions with the teaching staff, these discussions being part of the cue-seeking process. University and college teachers who have made their course objectives clear to students may well wish to encourage more students to adopt an active cue-seeking approach.

3.2.4. Personality Factors

A rather different line of research has been undertaken by Smith (1977), who used a forced-choice questionnaire to allocate students and teachers to one of sixteen clusters of four personality characteristics. The characteristics are based on categories originally enunciated by Jung but developed at the University of Florida by Myers and Biggs, hence the instrument used for identifying the clusters of personality characteristics is called the Myers-Biggs Type Indicator or MBTI (Myers, 1962). Using the MBTI, Smith and his co-workers were able to describe a person on any combination of the following four dimensions:

1. Extraversion to Introversion

2. Sensing to Intuition

3. Thinking to Feeling

4. Judging to Perception

The definitions of each of the above terms do not matter for our present purposes; readers who are seeking further details may consult Smith's description of his work. Nevertheless the following quotation from Smith gives an indication of the importance he places on this research:

> The type indicator attempts to measure the ways people become aware of things - by sensing and intuition: and the way people judge things - by thinking and feeling. It is our contention that a college student learns most naturally out of the kind of perception and kind of judgment he prefers. If this is correct, then the most effective college teaching will be that which matches teaching methods to the student's preferred mode of perceiving and judging (his learning style). (Smith, 1977, p. 273)

Smith illustrates the above claim by referring to experiments comparing the achievement of students with different learning styles who had been taught by contrasting methods. In these experiments it was found, for example, that students who were classed as "sensing" prefer deductive teaching and objective examinations, whereas "intuitive" students prefer inductive teaching and a greater freedom in examinations.

It will be noted that Smith's results confirm the findings of Pask, who was mentioned earlier. Interesting as they are, the chances of being able to give university teachers and students a series of personality tests before allocating students to classes are quite remote. If, however, a teacher is aware of the fact that a typical class will contain students whose preferred learning styles vary, the teacher can use a number of different methods in order to match teaching styles to the range of student needs.

Diagnostic tests, which were mentioned earlier for identifying differences in background knowledge, could include items which help identify key personality variables so that if the number of enrolling students is large enough to permit more than one class to be formed, or if the one lecture group is being divided into a number of smaller groups for tutorials or discussions, some account could be taken of personality factors. The majority of teachers in higher education would need professional advice, preferably from someone with a background in educational psychology, before implementing such a scheme.

One of the advantages of interviewing all new students is that teachers can discover prospective students' special interests and reasons for enrolling in the course. This knowledge should be quite useful in the detailed planning of presentation and the setting of assignments. A rather extreme example will illustrate this point. If, in a particular optional unit in a law school, none of the students enrolled is preparing for a legal career, the teacher will almost certainly wish to illustrate the legal principles with different examples from those which would be used in a class of future legal practitioners. Where the class contains students with different reasons for undertaking the course, as is fairly normal in higher education, the easiest way for the teacher to cater for differing student needs is by giving the students more choice in project work, assignments or examination questions. The implications of such choice will be discussed in Chapter 6.

3.3. HELPING STUDENTS TO LEARN

At one stage, particularly in the 1960s and early 1970s. many universities and colleges demonstrated their commitment to a need for helping their students to learn more efficiently by establishing "Study Skills Centres" or at least supporting members of the Counselling or Academic staffs who wished to offer short courses designed to help students in essay writing or provide practice in rapid reading and improved comprehension. Some of the more traditional universities with an elitist philosophy opposed such activities on the grounds that students needing such help were not really suited to university studies.

Although this type of assistance is still available in many institutions, efforts to improve student learning have taken another direction altogether, using the findings of research into how students learn carried out mainly in Sweden, the United Kingdom and Australia. some of which was referred to above. Much of this research up to 1979 is described in a special issue of *Higher Education* that year. in which Hounsell (1979) reviews the research to date. A more recent review of this research will be found in Marton, Hounsell & Entwistle (1984).

Other recent investigations show that students are more likely to attempt to reproduce "factual" material if their workload is too great and they are given little or no say in the choice of content, while on the other hand, they can be encouraged to adopt a much more analytical approach if their teachers emphasise the process, rather than the content of learning (Ramsden, 1982, p. 4; Ramsden and Entwistle, 1981 pp. 380-381).

3.4. STUDENT BACKGROUNDS AND COURSE CONTENT

Some course designers recognise the value of building on students' prior knowledge. For example, Hounsell (1984, pp. 193-194) refers to an Open University course entitled "Third World Studies" in which students' pre-conceptions, which are possibly incorrect, are deliberately used as a starting point for developing a better understanding of what is meant by "Third World", "development" and "developing". Hounsell also cites Eraut, Mackenzie and Papps (1975) who described an Economics course at Sussex University where students are given current economic problems to discuss, such as "Should British Leyland workers be given a ten pounds per week rise in wages?" Other ways in which a teacher can take into account students' needs and interests will be mentioned in the next chapter.

Even where the content of a course is beyond the direct control of a university or college teacher it is possible to allow students to concentrate on some topics of interest to them, particularly in project work and essays. This will be discussed in Chapter 6.

4. CHOICE AND ORDERING OF CONTENT

Frequently when teachers are criticised for failing to spend sufficient time on a difficult topic, they justify themselves by saying, "I must cover all the content in the syllabus (or course outline)". Attempts to "cover the content" indicate two misapprehensions on the part of the teacher. In the first instance they suggest that the teacher is likely to emphasise the acquisition of knowledge to the possible exclusion of equally important attitudes or skills. "Covering the content" also implies that the teacher assumes that anything which is "covered" in lectures will be automatically learned by students and, conversely, that everything which the students are expected to learn must be presented first in a lecture. The dual emphasis on content (or knowledge) and lecturing overlooks the importance of those objectives which have to do with the development of attitudes and skills and the existence of other effective forms of teaching and learning.

4.1. SELECTING AREAS OF CONTENT

At the outset in this chapter one should stress a point made earlier (at the end of Chapter 2), that before a teacher who has the responsibility for designing a course *de novo* begins to select the areas of knowledge for inclusion in the course, the teacher must consider the aims and objectives, examples of which were given in Chapter 2.

The course planner ought to realise that the knowledge which is now considered to be important may not be regarded as such in a few years time. Two implications arising from this rather obvious statement are frequently overlooked by course planners. The first is that most of us are unable to predict with any degree of accuracy which details of the subject matter will be regarded as important in five to ten years time, let alone twenty to thirty years, yet we are preparing graduates who will hopefully still be benefitting from their college or university education over the next thirty to forty years. The second implication is that, because knowledge is increasing and old attitudes are changing, graduates must be even more capable than their counterparts of a few decades ago of learning new skills, acquiring new knowledge and determining what is important for them in the changes that are taking place during their professional careers.

Before designing any course in detail teachers would be well advised to keep in mind the increasing acknowledgement given to the demands and, many would claim, rights of students to have some say in the selection of topics. Such demands from students should be weighed against the legal position of most tertiary institutions. After all it is the institution which awards the degree or diploma. The community which recognises this award expects that certain standards will be maintained. This is not to say that student choice of topics for study would reduce the standard of a degree: in fact the opposite is more likely to occur. If students are to be given any substantial say about what they should be taught (apart from selecting pre-packaged courses from a handbook), it should be made clear to everyone concerned that standards are not being lowered.

Having thought about the three related issues of the changing nature of knowledge, the need for graduates to be able to assume responsibility for their own continuing education and the desirability of allowing students some say in the design of the course, the next major step for the course planner is to re-examine the objectives of the course with a view to determining the **minimum** requirements in knowledge and/or skills needed by students to achieve these objectives. The planner is now in a position to select from a number of topics, any of which would be suitable for inclusion in this particular course. Some of these will be taken by all students because the teacher believes that all will profit from the inclusion of these topics; other topics will be available for study in depth by smaller groups of students working in "syndicates" (see Chapter 5, Section 5).

Among the essential components which are thus chosen, the teacher may well have included some sections which, though quite familiar to one group of students, would in essence be new material to another group. For example, students commencing first year Physics in an Australian university have generally studied some Physics in the upper secondary school, although it is possible to enrol in Physics I with previous studies limited to mathematics and one or more of the other sciences. Even for those with previous knowledge of physics there will be quite a few students who have taken advantage of the range of courses available in upper secondary school to study topics like electronics, astronomy or light without ever studying the fundamental principles of mechanics. The teacher consequently has to decide whether to include in the compulsory section of the course the material on mechanics which is claimed to be essential for understanding most other areas of physics, to require those students who have not previously studied mechanics to take a bridging course in that field, or to provide alternative work for some students while the others are studying mechanics. Similar examples of "essential" topics from other subjects could doubtless be cited.

In making a selection of "essential topics" for inclusion in a given course a teacher needs to decide whether any topics tentatively listed for inclusion would be better left for a later course, assuming that the course in question is in an early part of a sequence; alternatively, the student could well study such a topic after graduation. The decision about leaving certain topics until later can only be taken after discussion with the teachers in charge of later courses, as they will wish to express views on whether the topics in question are essential pre-requisites for their courses and some consideration would also have to be given to the most logical sequencing of learning experiences.

One final matter to be taken into consideration in selecting content is the choice of a textbook and the availability of other reference or teaching material, matters which will be taken up in more detail in Chapter 5. The reason for mentioning texts and teaching materials now is to highlight the fact that it is often very convenient to plan a course around a particular text or limited set of references and if suitable reading is readily available, it may well determine both the selection and ordering of content.

4.2. SELECTING AN ORDER OF TREATMENT

A knowledge of how students learn at university level can ease the task of deciding what is likely to be the most effective order of presenting new topics or experiences. It is, however, important to note that not all the research on learning is relevant to understanding how students undertake their studies at a college or university. Gagné (1967, 1971, 1975), for example, identifies six to eight major kinds of learning, each of which requires a different set of conditions for optimal occurrence. I shall not attempt to describe each of these kinds and the accompanying conditions here but shall confine my description to the three kinds of learning which Gagné (1971) sees as more applicable to learning at college level, namely **concept learning**, **principle learning** and **problem solving**. He acknowledges that in certain specialised subjects such as foreign languages other kinds of learning are necessary. This would also be true in those subjects where students have to acquire manipulative skills.

Gagné (1975, p. 58) identifies two general categories of concepts, namely "concrete" and "definitional". He writes about **concrete concepts** in the following manner:

> The learned capability called concrete concept enables the individual to **identify** a class of objects, object qualities or relations by "pointing out" one or more instances of the class. ...... What is important is that the acquisition of a concrete concept enables the learner to identify .... the entire class of things by indicating one or two examples of the class.

Examples of "concrete concepts" from higher education include neurons, microprocessors, language, carbohydrates and parabolas.

Unlike concrete concepts, **defined concepts** cannot be identified merely by "pointing them out". A small number of examples are meaningless without a definition of that particular concept. Many examples of defined concepts may be found in higher education: e.g. culture, society, money, climate, evolution.

An implication for teachers is that when introducing new concepts to students it is important for the teacher to recognise whether the concept is "concrete" or "defined" so that he or she might know whether a definition is essential to the understanding of the new concept. In all cases it is helpful to provide students with examples, or better still, ask the students to suggest examples.

Principle learning is not directly defined by Gagné (1971), but it is clear from his other writings (e.g. Gagné, 1967) that he uses the terms "principle" and "rule" more or less synonymously. He shows how concepts may be manipulated by students using **rules**, about which he says:

> Rules as learned capabilities make it possible for the individual to respond to a **class** of things with a **class** of performance.
> (Gagné, 1975, p. 61, emphasis his)

Examples of rule learning from tertiary education include balancing chemical equations, solving algebraic expressions, using correct grammatical structures, and selecting appropriate statistical techniques.

4.2.1. Problem Based Learning

The need to require students to solve problems is generally accepted; problem solving forms a large part of the practical work in technological subjects, mathematics, the natural sciences and social sciences. Many teachers of languages and the humanities also use problems from time to time, particularly with postgraduate students. An advantage of a problem centred approach to course design is that it encourages students to relate and apply their learning of different concepts, principles and rules, sometimes moving beyond the boundaries of the discipline in which the problem was originally set.

Problem based curricula have been developed in a number of colleges and universities and many of these are described in the literature (e.g. Woods, 1983; Maddison, 1980; Engel and Clarke, 1979). They are particularly suitable for use in professional faculties such as Engineering, Law, Education and Medicine. Woods (1983, pp. 81-83) compares the approach to problem solving of "novices" and "experts" and suggests a set of procedures which he has found to be successful at McMaster University, Ontario, for developing problem solving skills. In the present context it is sufficient to remind readers that many essay topics are stated in the form of problems and of course problems are used extensively in most science subjects. The three questions which are reproduced below illustrate this use of problems in stimulating students to learn.

- Evaluate the advantages and disadvantages of any possible spelling reform of present day English. (English, University of Lancaster, 1981)

- Individual socio-economic-political systems are said to be exemplified by different types of social stratification and mobility. Analyse, with reference to at least one Western and one Eastern European country, how far these different types can be observed in actual practice. (European Studies, University of Lancaster, 1981)

- Consider the role of population migration in shaping patterns of social and economic activity in early-modern England. (Geography, University of Lancaster, 1981)

Gagné also refers to a need for what he calls **cumulative learning**, and claims that the ability to learn new material depends very much on prior learning.

There is a specifiable minimal prerequisite for each new learning task. Unless the learner can recall this prerequisite capability (or some other which can serve the same purpose) he cannot learn the new task. (Gagné, 1971, p. 308)

Thus it should be possible, he claims, to designate for each learning task a set of concepts or principles which must be mastered or problems which must be solved before a new learning task can be undertaken. Despite the apparent simplicity of the above claim, Gagné asserts that many teachers do not keep this principle in mind when planning a course.

Another psychologist whose work is most relevant to the task of deciding an effective order of treatment is Ausubel (1963 and 1967). Like Gagné, he stressed that school (and by implication, college) learning is meaningful and therefore differs from the type of learning which had been previously studied under experimental conditions. In Ausubel's view, new materials presented to students for learning are only **potentially meaningful**. It is not until the student has integrated the new material with the old in an organised fashion and is able to use and recall that new knowledge with ease that meaningful learning has taken place. Implications for course planners are again clear: they must find ways of establishing links between the new subject material and that learnt earlier. This will be discussed in more detail in Chapter 5.

Ausubel (1963) postulates that for the most effective meaningful learning to occur certain conditions must be met. The first of these is a need for what he terms an **advance organizer**, namely that when a teacher is introducing a new topic, it is important to provide the students with information or experiences which will enable them to "bridge the gap between what the learner already knows and what he needs to know before he can successfully learn the task at hand." (Ausubel, Novak and Hanesian, 1978, pp. 171-2) This is most frequently done by means of a statement at the beginning of a lecture, but it may also be achieved by means of preliminary assignments or laboratory or field work. A second condition for effective learning is termed by Ausubel a **progressive differentiation of content**, about which he says:

> New ideas and information can be efficiently learned and retained only to the extent that more inclusive and appropriately relevant concepts are already available in cognitive structure to serve a subsuming role or to furnish ideational anchorage. (Ausubel, 1963, p. 79)

In the above rather concise statement, Ausubel appears to be saying that a learner needs to link each new idea or concept to a more comprehensive or general principle which already forms part of the student's repertoire of knowledge or skills.

The principle of progressive differentiation reinforces and possibly restates Gagné's principle of cumulative learning which was described above. Again it draws attention to the need for teachers when planning their courses to consider how they might relate each new section of the course to their students' previous experiences. If it is likely that students lack the necessary prior knowledge or experience it is then the responsibility of the teacher to see that they acquire it, by incorporating some new requirement in the pre-requisites for the course, by setting pre-reading or an introductory assignment before certain topics or by including the requisite knowledge and experiences in the main teaching program.

A third principle enunciated by Ausubel is **consolidation**.

> By insisting on consolidation or mastery of ongoing lessons before new material is introduced, we make sure of continued subject-matter readiness and success in sequentially organized learning. (Ausubel, Novak and Hanesian, 1978, p. 197)

Here one is reminded of the insistence on mastery in many "Keller plans" and computer assisted learning programs, about which more will be said in Chapter 5.

The fourth of Ausubel's principles which is relevant in planning tertiary courses is called **integrative reconciliation**, by which he means that when new material is learned, it is not only incorporated into the student's existing framework of knowledge but that some of the previously learned concepts will be modified as a result of the new learning. To quote one example from Ausubel, Novak and Hanesian (1978, pp. 124-5), students of Botany learn that tomatoes and beans are fruits in the botanical sense, hence their previous understanding of "fruit" is now modified. Teachers need to be aware of possible sources of confusion such as this and should avoid ambiguities. This need is particularly important in disciplines which attempt to give precise meanings to everyday terms such as "fruit" in Botany, "culture" in Sociology, and "argument" in Computing.

The following quotation summarises Ausubel's principles of the need for material to become meaningful before it can be learned, for it to be integrated with previous learning and for the student to organise all his or her learning into a hierarchy of inter-related concepts and principles.

> New meanings are therefore acquired when potentially meaningful symbols, concepts, and propositions are related to and incorporated within cognitive structure on a nonarbitrary, substantive basis. Since cognitive structure itself tends to be hierarchically organized with respect to level of abstraction, generality, and inclusiveness, the emergence of most new meanings reflects the

subsumption of potentially meaningful symbolic material under more inclusive ideas in existing cognitive structure. (Ausubel, 1967, p. 217)

4.3. ALLOCATION OF TIME FOR EACH TOPIC

Once the course planner has determined what topics will be included in the syllabus and the order in which they will be treated, the next step is to make a provisional allocation of time for each section of the course. It would obviously be foolish to plan for equal amounts of time for every topic, yet if this is the first occasion on which the teacher has organised such a course there may be no experience on the basis of which a judgment may be made about time needs for each section.

If a course planner lacks the necessary personal experience, the normal reaction is to make provisional allocations based entirely on the experience of colleagues or on the teacher's own estimate, with the proviso that adjustments will be made to the timing in the light of experience in the current course. There are, however, dangers in following this procedure in that topics listed for treatment early in the course may require much more time than was originally planned. As a consequence the teacher runs out of time for later topics which may be more important. The problem is similar to that met in planning a single lecture.

In the absence of personal experience or advice from others regarding allocation of time, the most pragmatic approach for the teacher is to consider carefully the specific objectives for each section of the course and the means by which students are expected to achieve these objectives. The planner is then in a better position to estimate the time required for each section even though some adjustment will probably be necessary before the end of the course. In order to provide for this adjustment and also to allow sufficient time to present important topics that are scheduled for later, the teacher should provisionally program some optional work which can be dropped if time does not permit its treatment. This may consist of new topics which are related to the general theme of the course, but it is better for the optional work to be an extension of one or more of the topics already in the course. The students would have been given an outline of the course upon enrolment and any deviation from this outline would give the appearance of breaking faith.

4.4. PREPARING THE COURSE OUTLINE

The last task which has to be completed before the course begins is the preparation of a statement which will indicate to students what they may expect in the course. The length of the outline will depend partly on whether it is to be printed in a *Faculty Handbook* a considerable time before the course begins, or in a more modest publication with a title such as *Students' Guide to Graphology AO1* which is prepared a few weeks before the beginning of term. As the two types of publication serve quite distinct purposes. the former being to guide students in the selection of courses and the latter for issue to students after they have enrolled, it is to be expected that they will contain different amounts of detail - the *Students' Guide* will be longer.

Both outlines will contain statements about pre-requisites or levels of knowledge which will be assumed at the beginning of the course. Both will also describe the aims of the course, but the listing of specific objectives could be confined to the *Students' Guide*.   Topics would merely be listed in the *Faculty Handbook*, whereas in the *Students' Guide* it would be desirable to elaborate slightly on each topic, either by including some sub-topics or including a one or two sentence description of each topic.

In the case of required and recommended readings, it is sufficient for the *Faculty Handbook* to list the set textbook(s) and indicate whether students are expected to read more widely than the text. The *Students' Guide*, on the other hand should tell students exactly what reading is expected and should list all texts and references, indicating any which are optional. It should be noted that it is usually the teacher's responsibility to let the bookshop know what texts are being prescribed and to inform the library if certain books or journals are likely to be in heavy demand. It goes without saying that these contacts with bookshop manager and librarian should be made well in advance of the commencement of an academic year.

The *Students' Guide* will also contain full details of the assessment system for the course, preferably including all the necessary information for any essays or other assignments which will be set. Some teachers may prefer to wait until the course has been running for a while before giving out essay topics or assignments, but there should be sound educational reasons for such a delay. For example, there are times when the premature revelation of an assignment or essay topic would interfere with earlier learning by the student in that students must complete certain work before they can be given a new problem to solve. In the *Faculty Handbook*, only a general indication of the type of assessment need be given, namely whether students will be given any choice and the proportion of marks to be allocated for examinations and for each assignment.

The place of assessment in course planning will be discussed in more detail in Chapter 6, but one other aspect of course design needs to be considered first, namely the selection of teaching methods which are appropriate to the aims and objectives of the course. This forms the basis of the chapter which follows.

5. SELECTION OF TEACHING METHODS

It should now be clear that the task of designing a university or college course is not complete once the subject matter has been selected and put into order. Part of the task of course design is to select the methods of teaching which are are most likely to result in maximum student learning, given the nature of the subject matter and the resources available to the teacher. In this chapter we shall examine briefly each of the main methods of teaching currently in use in tertiary education with a view to helping the reader decide which is the most appropriate for each section of any course which the reader is planning. As usual, references will be given to more extensive literature on the subject in order that the reader who is unfamiliar with a particular type of teaching may become better informed.

5.1. LECTURES

Basically, a lecture is a teaching session in which the teacher is the principal speaker. Although fifty minutes is the usual length of time for lectures, it is common practice to give a much shorter lecture, say ten minutes in length, at the beginning of a laboratory or workshop session. The degree of formality in lectures can be varied considerably to suit the audience, the occasion and the purpose of the particular lecture. A formal lecture may be defined as one in which the amount of verbal interaction between teacher and students is minimal, whereas an informal lecture may be interspersed with questions and some discussion periods. With a small class, especially in the later years of college or university, it is generally more appropriate for the lecture to be delivered in an informal style.

5.1.1. Purposes of Lectures

It is important, when deciding whether a lecture is the most appropriate method of teaching, to understand which functions of teaching are best achieved by means of lectures. Despite their long tradition and widespread use, lectures have been much criticised as a form of teaching (e.g. Gibbs, 1983; Dressel and Marcus, 1982), yet research on university teaching has unequivocally shown that lectures are well suited to achieving some at least of the objectives of university education (e.g. Bligh, 1972; Cockburn and Ross, 1977a and b). The following list summarises the main findings of research on the effectiveness of lectures, giving five purposes for which lectures are suitable and two key objectives for which the technique is unsuitable.

Lectures may be used effectively to:

1. present factual information and general principles in a cost-effective way;

2. survey the themes that unite various topics or aspects of the subject;

3. teach the application of a discipline's basic principles;

4. inform students of recent discoveries or new interpretations in the discipline;

5. demonstrate strategies and skills of problem solving.

Lectures have been shown, however, to be **not** as effective as discussions for:

1. changing attitudes;

2. enabling students to arrive at a deeper understanding of the subject.

5.1.2. The Place of Lectures in a Total Teaching Program

The first item in the above list of purposes for lectures uses the term, "cost-effective". When Bligh (1972, p. 17) states that "the lecture is as effective as other methods for transmitting information", there is a clear implication that if one were teaching only two or three students it may be better to select some other means of presenting information, but when classes consist of two or three hundred students, the lecture becomes very cost-effective. The exact point in class size at which lectures become cost-effective has not been determined, in fact I would suggest that it is impossible to make any general rule, for even with a class of one there could well be times when a lecture was warranted, namely when the teacher wishes to pass on information to the "class" which is not readily available elsewhere. At the opposite extreme there are occasions, as will be shown below, when some discussion can be organised in a very large class, even when the students are seated in a tiered lecture theatre.

It should be clear from the foregoing discussion that teachers who have sole responsibility for courses should think seriously about what they are trying to achieve and make conscious decisions on whether to use lecturing or some other form of teaching at each stage in the course.

5.2. DISCUSSIONS

The use of group discussion as a regular method of teaching is not at all new, yet it has become increasingly popular in almost all fields of higher education in recent years. It should be noted that the discussion method is not necessarily confined to tutorials or seminars; it may even have its place in a traditional lecture or science laboratory setting as will be shown below.

The value of using discussions as a regular feature of teaching and learning is described by Abercrombie (1979, p. 5) in the following extract (emphases hers):

> The group system of teaching focusses attention on the **interaction** between **all participants**, students and teachers, not on the polarized interaction of a student with a teacher. Like the tutorial, it recognizes individual differences, but goes further and not only allows for these differences, but actually exploits them. Exposed to the same display of information, each student has taken in not only different amounts, but different interpretations, and each learns by comparing and contrasting his uptake with that achieved by his peers. There is a network of communication between all members. In the tutorial set-up, the student's omissions and mistakes are corrected by the teacher: if the teacher is good, the student's store of information tends to match his teacher's in both content and organization. In the group system, the student discovers his strengths and weaknesses himself as he sees his behaviour in the light of others' and he modifies his attitudes or strategies as he sees that there are as many alternatives as there are members of the group.

It should be noted that in the above passage Abercrombie is distinguishing between two types of discussion sessions: a **tutorial**, in which one or two students are interrogated by the teacher and a **seminar**, where the focus is on discussion within a group of up to about sixteen students. Sometimes the terms "tutorial" and "seminar" are used interchangeably. It is preferable to confine the use of "tutorial" to a class where the emphasis is on the students' reactions to their reading and any difficulties difficulties they may have encountered. "Seminar", on the other hand, is a class where the emphasis is more on the subject matter being discussed, a distinction made, for example, by UTMU (1976, p. 54).

The importance of discussion as a means of stimulating student learning is emphasised by Cockburn and Ross who devote four of the nine small volumes in their very useful "Teaching in Higher Education Series" to this method of teaching and learning. (Cockburn and Ross, 1977c, d, e, f) They describe some of the advantages of discussion groups in the following terms:

In general terms small groups can **best** be used

1. to promote understanding of a body of knowledge and the relational thinking that this needs;

2. to elucidate misunderstanding and sort out students' difficulties;

3. to practise skills - intellectual, verbal, computational, social;

4. to practise the application of principles to familiar and unfamiliar situations;

5. to explore personal and professional attitudes and values;

6. as a two-way exchange of information on the teaching-learning process. (Cockburn and Ross, 1977e, p. 10)

Cockburn and Ross (1977e, p. 15) claim that tutorial groups may with profit focus their discussion on material which has been circulated earlier or on a task which group members have been asked to perform. Items which might form the basis for a "task-centred" discussion include:

- extracts from the text;

- a sequence of problems;

- lead-in lectures;

- video-tapes or films;

- preliminary mini-lectures;

- presentations by one or a group of students;

- models the group will work with;

- students' essays, papers, notes or translations;

- maps;

- sets of illustrations;

- folders or documents;

- research papers;

- prescribed preliminary reading. (*ibid*)

5.2.1. Using Discussions in Lectures

The technique of including short periods of discussion time within a formal lecture has been given the descriptive title, "buzz groups". Fuller descriptions of the technique are given by Bligh (1972, pp. 187-191) and McKeachie (1969, p. 23). At appropriate stages in a lecture, a teacher wishing to use buzz groups will ask the students to work in pairs, or sometimes groups of four, during which time they will discuss some problem that has been raised either by the lecturer or by one of the students. If necessary students turn around in their seats to form a group with students immediately behind them. At the end of a pre-announced time the teacher asks three or four of the groups to report on their discussion to the rest of the class; sometimes the main points are noted on the board or an overhead transparency, and other groups are invited to comment if their findings differ greatly from those which have been listed already. The buzz group technique has the advantage of breaking the lecture into more easily absorbed sections so that students can more immediately apply what they have just learned. In this way the lecturer is in the position of being able to identify and deal with any remaining problems.

5.2.2. Discussions in Science Practical Classes

Although informal discussions have always occurred between students working on joint practical projects, the inclusion of formal seminars and tutorials in undergraduate science courses is a much more recent phenomenon. Rudduck (1978, p. 6) reports that a meeting of physics lecturers produced the following list of reasons why group discussion should be used in learning physics: the comments in parentheses are hers. As Rudduck remarks, their list (and her comments) could well apply to many other subjects taught in universities.

1. To help students communicate as physicists. (This aim has to do with language, standards, the structure of knowledge.)

2. To provide practice in the application of principles.

3. To encourage the development of appropriate critical standards, and a questioning attitude to evidence.

4. To extend the range of ideas available to an individual. (It was suggested that the sum of the group's resources was greater than the sum of any individual's resources.)

5. To help students appreciate that physics is about people.

6. To provide an opportunity for students to clarify their thinking through talking (using the group as a critical sounding board).

7. To build opportunities for the critical examination of individual or sub-group assignments.

8. To encourage familiarity with significant achievements or achievers in physics.

5.2.3. Tutorial Discussions

As noted above, the word "tutorial" is used differently by different colleges and universities. Here we will concentrate on the tutorial as a class (preferably consisting of from six to sixteen students) where students are encouraged to discuss a problem which has arisen as a result of earlier course work. Rudduck (1978, pp. 15-16 and 32-33) claims that if a teacher is using tutorial discussions to change students' attitudes or give them a deeper understanding of the material being discussed, students should not be assessed on the quality (or quantity) of their contributions to group discussions. By thus removing any threat of penalty for remarks which the tutor might think are inappropriate or inadequately thought out, students are likely to feel less inhibited about participating and are therefore more likely to share their ideas and their difficulties.

Against this view that participation in tutorial discussion should not be assessed is the argument sometimes put by students that if they are expected to spend time in preparing for tutorials, they should be given some credit for this preparation in terms of marks. One useful answer to this real dilemma is described by Rudduck (1978, p. 39), namely that although students will not be assessed on the basis of their participation in tutorials they will be required to provide the tutor with evidence of their preparation by submitting notes on their reading for each tutorial. The tutor will write comments on these notes and keep a record of whether students have submitted material for each tutorial. Students who do not comply with the requirement to supply evidence of their reading will be penalised in the final assessment.

5.2.4. Seminar Discussions

In the sense that I have defined seminars it is probably true to say that they are used more frequently in postgraduate education or for sharing the results of recent research than in normal undergraduate courses. This may be due to a mistaken belief that undergraduates are not capable of expressing informed judgments on a research program or research findings. Perhaps it is better to limit the number of seminars planned for a normal undergraduate course, particularly if the number of enrolments is high, and seek student reactions to recent research or their interpretations of events or literature through essays.

5.2.5. Matching Type of Discussion to Students' Stages of Development

In the table which follows, Cockburn and Ross (1977f, p. 8) show how various types of groups at particular stages in a university or college course can be used to assist students with their progression through the stages of intellectual and ethical development originally identified by Perry (1970).

TABLE 5.1

A Development Plan for Small Group Teaching

Point of Transition	Perry's View of Students' Attitudes to Learning and to Knowledge	Form of Small Group
School to University	Right versus Wrong. Learning consists of finding "Right Answers". Teacher is "Authority".	Structured Group.
Some time during first or second years	Students perceive diversity of opinion without accepting its legitimacy. Is knowledge incomplete? Is academic knowledge strictly "academic"? If answers not right or wrong, what are standards for assessment?	Syndicates.
Second or third year perhaps	Diversity and uncertainty allowed to be legitimate - knowledge can be personal, contextual; personal ideas can be right. Is this a realm opposed to Authority or does Authority wish them to see things like this?	Associative discussion groups; tutorless groups developing into laboratory tutorials.
Second and subsequent years	All knowledge and values are contextual. Accept qualitative, relativistic element in reasoning. Rigorous examination of defined areas may become attractive.	Seminars or tutorless group. Laboratory tutorial.
Final year, honours or post-graduate classes	Recognise need to take up a position; personal orientation in field of knowledge.	Advanced seminar.

5.3. READING

Although in all tertiary courses, students are expected to do some reading, it would be fair to say that many university and college lecturers do not really expect their students to learn from their reading unless that reading is accompanied by some formal teaching, preferably in lectures. This belief shows itself in the endeavours of lecturers to "cover" every topic listed in the syllabus or course outline and the expectation on the part of the students that they will not be examined on anything which has not been "covered" in lectures. Such attitudes lead to treatment of some topics at quite superficial levels, with subsequent confusion on the part of students, increased work for tutors and poor performance in essays and examinations. If it were made clear to students at the beginning of a course that an important aim of higher education is for students to take responsibility for their own learning, that they will be expected to learn directly from their reading (and laboratory or field work where applicable) and that they may be tested on any topic listed in the syllabus, certain advantages would follow. There would be more time in lectures to examine certain issues in some depth or even to introduce new topics which would enhance students' understanding of the principles being taught, without a feeling that they were being disadvantaged because all topics had not been "covered". Examples could be found in many disciplines where an event which is reported in the media could be discussed with profit in lectures or tutorials, thus helping students to gain a better understanding of the more general principle which is illustrated by the media report. Examples of events with implications for disciplines in higher education include new discoveries in the sciences, new applications in technology, new laws and regulations, and budgetary announcements.

In order to put into effect the suggestions being made here, the person in charge of a course should include a statement in the course outline and in the first lecture that, by the end of the course, students are expected to demonstrate the acquisition of certain knowledge and skills (these should be listed in the course outline), and the ability to learn directly from their reading, and they will be expected to show evidence of this reading in their essays, tutorial worksheets and final examinations. The above statement will need to be supported with a list of books or articles recommended for reading, with some indication as to the relative importance of the various items and also an indication of the amount of reading that is expected.

5.3.1. Reading Lists

The dangers of confusing students by giving them too long a reading list are pointed out in UTMU (1976, pp. 67-69). The UTMU team suggests a structure for reading lists which would aid students in their choice of material for study by indicating relative degrees of importance for each item in the list. The writers suggest that items in lists should be grouped into categories in the following way:

1. one or two items of introductory reading;

2. one or two texts for the course (if they exist);

3. further and more advanced reading (books or papers), perhaps broken down by topic to aid in clarity and selection;

4. important primary and original sources;

5. essential reference works, and

6. any other miscellaneous publications the teacher thinks are worth mentioning. (UTMU, 1976, p. 68 with slight alterations to the wording)

The UTMU writer also reminds lecturers of a need to inform the library and bookshops of likely demands by students for books and journals in the list. The library may need to put some items on restricted borrowing and the bookshop needs time to order sufficient copies for students to purchase at the beginning of term.

5.4. PRACTICAL EXPERIENCES

With the possible exception of Mathematics courses, it is almost inconceivable to envisage a program leading to a first degree in Science, Engineering, Medicine or allied fields that does not have a substantial practical component. A rationale for making laboratory work compulsory in science and technology courses is not hard to find, yet there are many accounts of students' complaints about practical work being "boring and a waste of time" (Ogborn, 1977, pp. 2-4).

5.4.1. Aims of Practical Work

UTMU (1976, p. 75) list seventeen of the most common reasons for including a practical component in university courses. At least ten of these could be achieved by other methods; those which are the most compelling reasons for compulsory laboratory classes in certain courses are:

- (3) to develop manipulative skills;

- (4) to familiarise students with instruments and apparatus;

- (5) to familiarise students with the design and construction of experimental equipment;

- (6) to develop observational skills;

- (7) to develop skills in gathering and interpreting data.

The UTMU team's list is followed by a warning that "there are two prior questions which might be asked in respect of these aims: is their achievement an essential part of the course? and are there more economic or effective ways of achieving them?" (*ibid*). If these questions were to be taken seriously by course planners, much of the present student dissatisfaction with laboratory classes would be eliminated. There would undoubtedly be substantial savings in time and resources which could be put to more effective use elsewhere.

5.4.2. Sequencing of Laboratory Experiences

Lack of sufficient equipment for large first year classes sometimes makes it impossible for all students to follow the same sequence of experiments in practical classes, desirable as this may be from a pedagogical viewpoint. An alternative, frequently favoured in Physics laboratories, is to provide two or three experimental kits and sets of instructions for each experiment in the program. Students, usually working in small teams, may do the experiments in any order, provided a kit is available. If such a system is adopted, it is desirable to allow students the choice of completing say eight out of ten of the available experiments.

Two problems arise when the above method of organisation is adopted. First, there is an implicit assumption that although students are expected to improve their manipulative, observational and analytical skills as they progress through a series of experiments, the order in which the Physics (or other science content) is encountered does not matter. Such an assumption is patently false. One response to this problem is to select experiments which do not require an advanced level of knowledge in the subject, but this restriction would place unacceptable limits on the benefits which can be gained from practical work, especially in the ability to test applications of theoretical principles.

A more acceptable response to this first problem is to indicate to students that although there is no fixed sequence for completing experiments in the program, certain experiments requiring higher levels of knowledge may only be performed after students have demonstrated their knowledge of related theory, either by means of a short diagnostic test or by presenting a satisfactory laboratory report of an experiment which is deemed to provide a suitable introduction to the one in question.

A second problem is associated with the relative difficulty of the experiments, both in terms of time required for completion of each experiment and the level of analytical thought demanded. It is impossible for experiments to be designed in such a way that they will be equally difficult for all students and so that the degree of difficulty will not be affected by the order in which the students perform the experiments. Thus it becomes necessary for the teacher in charge of the practical work to use some system of weighting when marking a student's report of laboratory work in order to allow for inherent difficulties, such as the amount of time expected and the level of conceptual skills required. If the teacher expects students' performance to be better if the experiment is performed later rather than earlier in the course, an additional weighting will be needed to compensate for the timing of the experiment. The technique of weighting will be treated in greater depth in Chapter 6 together with other aspects of assessment.

The problems of making a limited amount of equipment available to a large class of students while retaining the concept of progressive or cumulative learning experiences are discussed by Ogborn (1977, p 73), who contrasts two approaches to the organisation of laboratory classes. Although both examples are at different levels in university Physics courses, the principles could be applied in other areas of tertiary science or technology teaching. In the first example Shonle (1970) required all first year Physics students to carry out certain basic measurements, the main aims being to ensure their familiarity with the equipment - aim (4) above - and their ability to interpret data - aim (7). Once students have demonstrated their basic proficiency they then use the equipment to carry out measurements or experiments of their own choice, thus achieving another of the aims listed by UTMU, namely

- (16) to develop personal responsibility and reliability for experimentation.

Ogborn's second example. which comes from Graetzer (1972). refers to an advanced course in Physics. Graetzer's laboratory has a number of different sets of equipment available and each group of students works with a different set for the first three week period. leaving a cumulative record of their experiences. Each group then moves to a second set of equipment but in using this they are guided by their own experience on the first set and the records of the group which used this equipment in the first three week period. The process is repeated. with records of successive groups of students (within the one class) being made available as each group moves on to more experiments. In such a way Graetzer makes it possible for students to learn from the experiences of their group and of the whole class.

5.4.3. Teamwork in Laboratory Planning

In the previous section reference was made to the teacher in charge of a science laboratory and examples were given of approaches used by two university teachers of Physics. Although it is a common practice to make one person responsible for laboratory classes associated with a given course (frequently the person in charge of the course), it is normal for this person to be assisted by technicians and demonstrators in running the laboratory. I mention the technical staff first because they must be consulted about the availability of apparatus and materials well before classes begin and they are also likely to be well aware of problems encountered by students using equipment for the first time. It is therefore helpful to include at least one member of the technical staff on any planning team for a course which includes practical work. (See also Ogborn, 1977, pp. 28-30)

Demonstrators (or Teaching Assistants) are either post-graduate students (very occasionally senior undergraduates), members of the academic staff of the department or graduates employed for this particular purpose (usually part-time). Even when they are not as well qualified academically as the lecturer in charge of the course, they are frequently better able to identify the difficulties commonly experienced by students in laboratory sessions. When demonstrators are members of the planning team they are more likely to have a strong sense of commitment to the course. Their greater awareness of the reasons for inclusion of each experiment will also assist them should they be asked to assess students' progress. Ogborn (1977, pp. 19-23) refers to a need for making demonstrators aware of what students are expected to gain from each experiment or observation, claiming that this is much more important than knowing what answers are expected.

5.4.4. Laboratory Notes and Instructions

Students are expected to develop initiative and resourcefulness as a result of their laboratory experiences (UTMU's aim 15) and ought therefore to be spared the boredom which results from a "cookery book" approach to practical work. The issued instructions should provide adequate guidance in order to avoid the wasting of time and damage to specimens or equipment, while at the same time acting as a challenge to students to use their prior knowledge and understanding of the subject when interpreting the results of the day's activity. When an element of experimental design can be included in the exercise as in the cases described by Shonle and Graetzer above, so much the better. Instructions or laboratory manuals which are too detailed will inhibit students' ability to learn from the practical activity. Some commercially prepared laboratory manuals written as supplements to textbooks manage to combine detailed directions and descriptions, where these are deemed to be necessary, with broader questions asking students to explain experimental data in the light of their theoretical knowledge of the discipline. Course books from The Open University in the United Kingdom also use this technique most effectively.

5.4.5. Field Work

Not all practical work is conducted in laboratories; field work is an important component in the biological sciences and their derivatives and in engineering. It often provides the student's only "practical experience" in the social sciences. One of the most important differences between laboratory and field work, apart from the location, is that it is much easier to control the variables in the laboratory, hence the results of observations or experiments are easier for the teacher to predict. In the "field" (or a community or industry) students have to contend with the effects of a very wide range of climatic or personality factors on the processes or objects they are asked to observe. "Personality factors" include any influence the student observers may have on the events they are studying, particularly when they are examining human or animal behaviour. When engaged in field work students may also suffer the disadvantage of having less direct contact with their teachers. While lack of contact with teachers can lead to greater student autonomy, it may have the undesirable result that inexperienced students fail to make vital observations in the field.

5.5. SYNDICATES AND GROUP PROJECTS

The value of group discussion was described in the quotation from Abercrombie (1979) at the beginning of Section 5.2 and very brief reference was also made to group work in laboratory classes. In the present section the emphasis will be on students working together on a task which may be set by the teacher or chosen by the group itself. Such tasks include:

1. preparing a report on field work in one of the earth sciences, social sciences or biological sciences;

2. writing a script for a film in one of the humanities or social sciences;

3. presenting arguments for and against some theory in philosophy or religion;

4. designing a structure in architecture or engineering;

5. suggesting a sequence of diagnostic tests followed by treatment for a patient with specified symptoms in medicine.

Whereas in discussion groups or in laboratory team work the emphasis is on a relatively short-term task or problem, a syndicate has a much longer project to complete. The type of learning task which is best suited to a syndicate is one which would be difficult or too time-consuming for a student to undertake alone, where each member of a syndicate team can contribute special skills, and where these contributions from individual members are regarded by the team as potentially equally valuable. During syndicate learning the teacher's role changes from being mainly didactic to one which is consultative or advisory (UTMU, 1976, p. 80).

Performance in syndicates is normally assessable, thus creating problems for the teacher in deciding how to allocate marks or grades to members of each syndicate group. Techniques for assessing group projects will be described in Chapter 6.

5.6. INDIVIDUALISED LEARNING

The phrase "individualised learning" has several connotations. It places an emphasis on the work of one student rather than a syndicate or the class as a whole. It could refer to the practice of giving students greater autonomy in deciding what they will study and how they will be assessed. (See, for example, Prosser and Thorley, 1981; Tarrant, 1982) It is also used to describe a system of self-paced learning, usually attributed to Keller (1968), which will be described later, or to a scheme in which students learn at their own pace from a combination of tapes, slides and other materials, or audio-tutorials, which will also be described later. Finally, with the assistance of computers, or some other forms of programmed learning, "individualised instruction" may indicate that the choice of topics, order of presentation, amount of explanation and examples and even modes of assessment are governed by each student's performance in an initial diagnostic test and modified in response to the student's performance in a series of progress tests after each new block of instruction. Readers interested in the experiences of university teachers who have given their students more autonomy in choosing the content and method of learning should consult Boud (1981).

5.6.1. Student Autonomy in the Selection of Content

It is clear from the action of many academics that their attitudes are ambivalent towards the idea of allowing students to choose what they will learn in a university or college course. Most academics, at least in the Western world, seem to support the principle that students who are beginning their tertiary education should be allowed to select whatever course of study they are capable of undertaking and qualified to enter, yet once the students have enrolled for a particular course, the same academics adopt a very rigid attitude towards their students' patterns of learning. This rigidity is even applied to the total pattern of courses leading to a degree, particularly when the degree leads to professional qualifications.

Perhaps one reason why teachers are unwilling to allow their students too much autonomy in the selection of content is that they are afraid that standards will be lowered. This problem was discussed at one of the seminars which formed part of the "Leverhulme Programme of Study into the Future of Higher Education" in the United Kingdom chaired by Professor Gareth Williams of the University of Lancaster (now at the University of London). Bligh (1982, p. 20) comments that even with more student autonomy it is still the teacher's responsibility to "set academic standards and encourage the patterns of thought that constitute their discipline". He makes the additional claim that a student centred approach can actually "raise academic standards by placing less emphasis upon the acquisition of information from lectures, books and other presentations" (ibid).

While the interests of professions in maintaining reasonable entry standards must be recognised in the selection of content for a professional degree, most university teachers would admit that many curricula leading towards such degrees contain content which is not really necessary for the satisfactory conduct of the profession, or even for understanding other relevant parts of the course. An illustration of this tenacity to include subjects or topics which are no longer relevant could, until recently, be found in some Pharmacy degree programs. Because pharmacists once had to prepare many of their own drugs from plants, it was essential that pharmacy students should gain a knowledge of Botany, particularly in the area of plant identification. That particular aspect of botanical studies disappeared from the pharmacy curriculum many years ago, yet Botany 1 was still compulsory in many pharmacy degrees.

Too great a control over course content, whether by the Faculty or a professional body, does not allow those who do the day-to-day teaching any freedom for modifying the course to take account of new discoveries or new directions in professional practice. As a consequence, teachers are less likely to allow their students freedom in selecting content. It should nevertheless be recognised that within every profession there are opportunities for specialisation and for using consultants from other sections of the profession when necessary. Most professions also recognise a need for post-graduate qualifications in the area of specialisation, so that "general practioners" in the field, whether they be family doctors, solicitors or accountants, need not, in their first degree, be expected to gain an in-depth understanding of material which is only necessary for one branch of the profession. Additional reading, short courses or more advanced studies leading to a higher degree or fellowship may compensate for any omissions in the first degree.

5.6.2. Personalised System of Instruction (the Keller Plan)

This approach to course organisation is frequently called the Keller Plan after the man who first publicised the method after using it in his own teaching (Keller, 1968). Details of the plan were further elaborated by Keller and Sherman (1974) when it received the more descriptive title of Personalised System of Instruction or PSI. For accounts of more recent applications of PSI one should consult Brook and Thomson (1982), who developed a course in statistics, or Vaughan (1982) who developed a method of teaching chemistry to first year university classes using the Keller methods.

Individualised instruction allows students to determine (within limits set by the teacher) their individual rates of progress through a series of learning tasks. These tasks would have been prepared in advance by the teacher. When a student feels that he or she is ready to move to the next learning cycle, the student requests a test; in Keller's classes the test was administered by a senior student called a "proctor". Generally speaking the student is required to demonstrate "mastery" of the subject matter (or objectives for that cycle) before being allowed to proceed. Mastery is often defined as a score of at least 90 per cent in the progress test. but the level would be determined by the nature of the material learned.

5.6.3. Audio-Tutorials

At the beginning of this section reference was made to a scheme in which students learn at their own pace from a combination of tapes, slides and other materials. Postlethwait, who developed this method for teaching laboratory classes, called the system "audio-tutorials" (see Postlethwait, Novak and Murray. 1979; also Brewer, 1977). For successful operation it requires not only detailed preparation of written materials, microscope slides, projection materials, apparatus. chemicals and preserved specimens well before term begins, but also supplies of fresh specimens (if these are to be studied) over a longer period of time than would normally be the case. Experience in the Australian National University has shown that for the program to operate successfully over a period of years it is essential to have a dedicated person as chief tutor in charge of the laboratories who is available at most times of the day to answer student inquiries. It is also important to update the instructions and course materials at regular intervals.

5.6.4. Programmed Texts

During the early 1960s considerable effort was put into writing textbooks in the form of a series of questions, each of which required a correct response from students before they could proceed to the next question or item of information. The development of programmed texts was more or less parallel with that of teaching machines which were designed to ensure that students were forced to take an active part in their learning. These machines varied from quite simple boxes containing a roll of paper and a window which revealed one "frame" of information or questions at a time to more sophisticated electrically operated equipment which preceded computers. Two basic forms of programmed learning existed, namely linear and branching programs. In each case, students were only supposed to move on to the next step in the program when they had successfully completed the prior one. The main difference between linear and branching programs was that in the former the sequence of steps was fixed, whereas in the latter, the next step for a student would be determined by his or her answer to the preceding question. The system was designed to allow students to proceed at their own pace, but in most cases it failed to allow students with different background knowledge to learn in ways most suited to their needs, despite the optimistic claims of programmed learning designers.

Even so, Stones (1981), in a review of the programmed learning movement, claims that there were educationally sound programs written, but that machines as such were unnecessary, a programmed text or set of notes being successful. He claims (p. 9) that one reason for their lack of acceptance was that the philosophy of mastery learning which was inherent in most teaching programs was incompatible with normative assessment. ("Mastery learning" generally implies that a student must score 90% on 90% of the questions for successful progress, whereas "normative assessment" suggests that about two-thirds of the students in a class will score within one standard deviation of the class mean which is probably at about the 60% level.)

A more recent case of successful programmed learning is described by Tarrant (1982) who developed programmed learning materials for teaching Economics and Commerce at the University of Bath. He reports that students using programmed materials performed better than students taught by conventional methods, that commerce students were more favourably disposed towards the programmed instruction than were the economics students, and that this form of instruction was reasonably cost-effective even though its cost was higher than conventional teaching (*ibid* pp. 144-5).

5.6.5. Computer Assisted Learning

Computer assisted learning or instruction (CAL or CAI) developed from the earlier forms of programmed instruction. It is sometimes confused with computer managed learning (CML), the main difference being that the former is a method of presenting new material to a student and usually testing the student's acquisition of the new knowledge, whereas the latter is a system for keeping records of student progress, which may include tests, and usually recommends remedial exercises or consultations if a student is not performing adequately. There are many publications describing the variations of CAL and CML; the journal *Programmed Learning and Educational Technology* frequently describes uses of these techniques in higher education and the *World Yearbook of Education* 1982/83: *Computers in Education* edited by Megarry *et al.* (1983) contains a number of short descriptions of CAL and CML in about six countries. An important advantage of using computers for programmed instruction is that the computer ensures that students are prevented from moving on to the next step if they fail to master the previous one, and branching programs are made much more manageable.

Unfortunately many CAL programs have not advanced beyond the better programmed textbooks as they fail to make best use of the capabilities of a computer. Both Hoyle (1983) and Howe (1983) question the viability of many current CAL programs. Hoyle, for example, compares the use of computers in classrooms with other innovations such as the Initial Teaching Alphabet and educational television (p. 57). He refers to the many extravagant claims and predictions made for these and reminds readers that quite a few items of expensive equipment purchased as part of the new methods of teaching are now gathering dust on the shelves of classrooms or school store-rooms. He describes a number of reasons commonly given by teachers for failing to adopt innovations (p. 59), including lack of familiarity with the operation and capabilities of the equipment. Howe adds another reason which is particularly germaine to CAL (p. 71), namely that most CAL programs compare the answers given by students with a range of sample answers supplied by the writer of the program, thus depriving students of any opportunities for creative writing or, for that matter, the teacher the opportunity for interpreting and clarifying unusual or unexpected answers.

The answer to these criticisms is not to reject CAL, but for teachers to be more selective in their use of computers in teaching. There now exist quite a few "author languages" which enable teachers to write their own programs for use on either mainframe or microcomputers, but the time needed for preparing really challenging programs for use in higher education is quite high and may be beyond the financial resources of some institutions.

With the availability of many good word-processing programs on micro and main-frame computers, students are increasingly using computer facilities for statistics, engineering and architecture (to name just a few subjects which regularly use computers in undergraduate teaching). It is also pleasing that some lecturers in the humanities encourage their students to write essays or poetry on the computer, making full use of the word processing facilities, such as repositioning a section of the text or inserting or deleting words or phrases. (The writing of this book has been greatly facilitated by having access to VAX computers, first in Lancaster University in the United Kingdom and then in the Australian National University.)

Additional benefits to be gained from using computers in teaching are listed below:

- random numbers may be generated in order to vary the details of questions containing numerical data, thus ensuring that every student is asked a different set of questions;

- random numbers may also be used to select from an item bank a number of terms which the student is asked to define;

- in subjects such as engineering and accountancy the CAL can include complex calculations which are performed by the computer, thus giving the student instant feedback on whether the right method has been chosen;

- complex situations may be simulated in disciplines as far afield as astronomy, marketing, chemistry, pharmacology, political science and engineering.

5.7. DISTANCE EDUCATION

The term "Distance Education" refers to what were once called correspondence courses, the change in name being possibly related to the fact that whereas in the older type courses, communication between teacher and student was almost entirely by mail, in today's courses the mail is only one of many means of communication between teachers and external students. A comprehensive treatment of distance education including course planning, design of instructional materials, arrangements for meetings with students and provision of feedback is well beyond the scope of this book. Among the many descriptions of experiences with this mode of teaching are articles by Daniel (1983) and Lamy and Henri (1983). The former describes some of the general principles and practices; the latter describes the operation of a particular system in the Province of Quebec. Institutions planning to offer courses to external students would be well advised to spend some time at one of the places which specialises in this activity, the best known of which is the Open University at Milton Keynes in the United Kingdom. Australian universities have endeavoured for many years to cater for the scattered population in this country and have consequently built up considerable experience in distance education. The main university centres for distance education (or external degrees) in Australia are the University of Queensland in Brisbane, the University of New England in Armidale, N.S.W.; Murdoch University in Western Australia; and Deakin University in Geelong, Victoria. Quite a few Colleges of Advanced Education and Institutes of Technology also provide for external students.

In addition to printed materials which are sent through the mail and specially designed texts which students are expected to purchase, other forms of communication between institutions and their students include telephone facilities for students to keep in touch with each other and their tutors, audio-visual materials such as video-cassettes or audio-cassettes with accompanying photographs or diagrams. Floppy discs are increasingly being used on microcomputers in students' homes or at a centralised study centre. Hooper (1983) gives a number of examples of computers being used to enhance distance education and distinguishes between a system which depends on sending floppy discs through the mail and a more interactive system where the students' terminals are in direct contact with a large computer at the university, usually through telephone lines, although the link could be through a satellite. When students have direct access to the university's computer they are more likely to be interacting with a computer program than with a tutor on another terminal, although the latter is technically possible, but supposedly more costly.

6. MEASURING PROGRESS AND ACHIEVEMENT

An essential part of course development is planning for the measurement of students' progress at regular intervals and for assessing the final levels of achievement. Traditional ways of making these measurements include the use of essays, laboratory exercises, problems and, of course, tests and examinations. In this chapter we shall consider some of the advantages and disadvantages of different forms of assessment and suggestions will be made about the design of tests, the wording of essay questions, the marking and the interpretation of results.

6.1. SOME EDUCATIONAL ROLES OF ASSESSMENT

Feletti (1980)[*] lists eight important functions which assessment systems are designed to achieve. Although his list was developed in the context of an undergraduate medical program, it has general applicability and is therefore reproduced here.

Any student assessment should:

1. provide students with opportunities to demonstrate **application** of knowledge, attitudes or skills where appropriate, and not just the recall of information;

2. test for problem-solving and problem-management as the most important applications, beside the use of the underlying sciences in justifying decisions;

3. allow students who can complete learning tasks earlier to proceed with elective studies (to follow their own interests, and promote independent learning), but at the same time

4. allow the other students more time and guidance to achieve competence without the problem of intervening (new) learning tasks;

5. provide rapid knowledge of the results, with an emphasis on diagnostic information to allow students to monitor their own progress and plan remedial studies;

6. be an open system, where standards are known. and where the required levels of competence are stated beforehand;

7. encourage assessment of their own and their peers' performance as a means towards their own further education through observation, discrimination and decision-making;

8. encourage students to carefully evaluate this and other aspects of the educational programme, towards their future skills in adapting to and fostering change responsibly. (*loc. cit.* pp. 170-171)

* From *Higher Education*, Vol 9, 1980, Elsevier, Amsterdam; by permission of Martinus Nijhoff Publishers Dordrecht, The Netherlands

6.2. ABILITY, PROGRESS AND ACHIEVEMENT

The terms **diagnostic, formative** and **summative** have been used by various authors to describe three quite different types of assessment. Bloom, Hastings and Madaus (1971), for example, describe in some detail the use of these different types of measures for a range of school subjects. The general principles which they enunciate are, however, quite applicable to university or college teaching.

Diagnostic measures are designed to identify each student's strengths or weaknesses, sometimes in order to determine who will be admitted to a course and who will be directed to a different type of course or remedial program. At other times they will be used to guide the teacher in planning or modifying the content or mode of presentation to better suit the needs of students. Evidence based on students' performance in pre-requisites, such as final high school examinations, can be quite misleading. It is generally too global and does not provide sufficiently detailed information about specific abilities, knowledge, and weaknesses of individual students. Thus diagnostic measures may take the form of short tests (often multiple-choice) or essays, usually set at the beginning of a course or a section of a course. When classes are small enough it is often sufficient for the tutor to interview individual students and thereby estimate each student's ability in the subject.

Formative measures of progress are designed to provide information which will indicate to students the extent of their progress in a course and thus guide them in their learning. Formative assessment frequently gives students practice in skills such as essay writing, computation and problem solving, drawing or the operation of equipment. It is preferable that any marks given for formative tasks should only be allowed to influence a student's final result in a minor way, if at all, as it is the student's final level of achievement in a subject which is the most important.

One of the chief problems with what is known as "continuous assessment" arises when formative assessment is allowed to dominate all other teaching and learning activities. to the extent that students do not have time to pursue reading in depth, or even to maintain a healthy balance between academic, social and recreational activities. Furthermore the teaching staff are kept so busy setting and marking tests and essays that they have little or no time for engaging in research.

Summative assessment may be defined as a measure of a student's performance or level of achievement at the end of a sequence of study. This measure may be used to certify that a student has reached a desirable level of competence or that the student is qualified to proceed to more advanced studies. It should be noted that summative measures are not confined to the end of a course: consequently it is quite legitimate to use some summative measures at appropriate stages within a course. The difficulty is to decide what should be regarded as summative and what is formative, and thus the extent to which each earlier or interim measure is allowed to influence the final grade. This raises the problem of allocating suitable weights to each item of assessment, an issue which will be discussed later in this chapter.

6.2.1. Use of Student Progress Measures for Feedback to Teacher

Reference has been made to the value of diagnostic tests and preliminary interviews in course planning and to the value of formative measures for guiding the student. It is clear that the results of any progress tests and an analysis of students' performance in essays given relatively early in a course will also be of great value to the teacher. They will indicate whether a significant proportion of the class is having difficulty with particular tasks, in which case the teacher may have to arrange for remedial programs to be available. The teacher may also decide to change the pre-requisites for future entry to the course, or make changes in the content, order of treatment or mode of presentation.

When a majority of students have performed badly in a progress test or an essay set relatively early in the academic year, a conscientious teacher may wonder whether the marks for that work should be ignored or perhaps scaled upwards when being counted towards the final assessment score. To ignore the marks would penalise any students who put extra effort into this first piece of work, yet it hardly seems fair to penalise the major part of a class for an error of judgment on the part of the teacher. Increasing the marks of all students, on the other hand, can result in the weaker students being credited with knowledge or skills which they did not possess, at least at the time of the essay or test. The best compromise would therefore appear to be to allow those students who have done well in the initial work to count their early scores towards their final grades, but to base the final grades of other students on their performances later in the course. No simple formula will allow a teacher to be fair to all students; final judgments about grades will invariably include a subjective element.

6.3. KNOWLEDGE, SKILLS OR ATTITUDES?

It has long been recognised that education is not limited to increasing students' knowledge. Teachers at all levels, from kindergarten to university, are also interested in developing in their students certain skills and attitudes which either the teacher or society regards as important. During the 1950s and 1960s attempts were made to describe in systematic ways the different categories and levels of learning. This search coincided with a movement which emphasised the need for teachers to be more specific in stating what they hoped to achieve by their teaching (see, e.g. Chapter 2, also Blishen, 1969 and Mager, 1962).

The best known of these schemes was suggested by Bloom (1956) and his colleagues and later expanded by Krathwohl et al. (1964), an original member of the Bloom team, and Simpson (1966). According to these authors, there are three broad categories of educational objectives or desired outcomes of learning and within each category from five to six major levels may be identified. These categories they call "domains" and the three are the Cognitive, the Affective and the Psychomotor. **Cognitive** objectives are those dealing with the acquisition and use of knowledge; **Affective** are those which refer to attitudes and value judgments, and **Psychomotor** refer to manipulative skills. The above-mentioned researchers developed a set of "Taxonomies" or systems of hierarchical classification which took into account the existence of higher and lower orders of objectives.

In higher education much more attention has been given to the cognitive domain than the other two, and a more recently proposed fourth domain, the **Perceptual** (Moore, 1967), is seldom mentioned in the literature. Even so, a chapter by T.S. Baldwin in Bloom, Hastings and Madaus (1971) describes how all four domains are relevant to courses in industrial education, which would be taught mainly in Colleges of Technical and Further Education in Australia.

6.3.1. Levels of Cognitive Objectives

Bloom *et al.* (1956) refer to six levels of objectives in the cognitive domain, namely:

Knowledge ability to recall specific items of information, to describe known ways of dealing with this information, or to enunciate previously learned general priniciples or theories;

Comprehension ability to demonstrate one's understanding by translating or paraphrasing, interpreting information or extrapolating from given data in order to determine likely implications or effects;

Application ability to apply abstract principles to particular and concrete situations;

Analysis clarification of a complex situation by breaking it down into its constituent parts, identifying any relationships between the parts, and identifying any organizational structure inherent in the original situation or set of data;

Synthesis bringing together a number of facts or ideas to create a new pattern or structure such as a unique communication, a proposed set of operations or a set of abstract principles which are derived from the original data;

Evaluation judgments about the value of materials or methods for a given purpose. (after Bloom, Hastings and Madaus, 1971, pp. 271-273)

The above system allows teachers to classify the level of objectives being sought when teaching programs are being planned and is particularly helpful when a teacher is designing a test. Since the taxonomy was developed many examples have been given in the literature of test questions suitable for assessing the levels students have reached in their learning (see e.g. Bloom, Hastings and Madaus, 1971). It should be noted that not all types of test question are equally suitable for testing the different levels of objectives. Essay questions are suitable for assessing comprehension, application and evaluation. Recall of factual knowledge is tested by short answer questions while analytical ability lends itself to being assessed by problems or exercises. Some course planners find it helpful to prepare a grid which shows the cognitive level being tested in each component of the assessment scheme. The grid may also indicate the spread of topics being tested and at what level; it sometimes includes objectives from the non-cognitive domains. The example of a grid in Table 6.1 indicates the cognitive levels which are usually (+) or occasionally (?) tested by various forms of assessment. Instead of the symbols in the body of the grid it would be possible to enter the topics or subtopics being tested.

Examples of these grids may be found in almost every chapter of Bloom, Hastings and Madaus (1971), and while the majority of these examples are from primary (elementary) or secondary (high) schools, the general principle is well illustrated.

TABLE 6.1

Matching Question Types to Levels of Objectives

	Knowl.	Compr.	Applic.	Anal.	Synth.	Eval.
Definitions	+	?				
Multiple Choice	+	+	+	?		?
Labelling Diagrams	+	?				
Interpreting Graphs	+	+	?	+		?
Explaining a Theory	+	+	?	?	?	?
Statistical Problems	+	+	+	+		+
Laboratory Exercises	+	+	+	+	?	?
Examination Essays	+	+	+	+	?	+
Term Essays	+	+	+	+	+	+
Thesis	+	+	+	+	+	+

As will be seen from Table 6.1, the most commonly used forms of assessment which measure students' ability to achieve the higher levels of synthesis and evaluation are major essays and theses. Sometimes this is also possible with examination essays (which typically take about 30 minutes to write). The following questions which appeared in recent examination papers at universities in Britain and Australia illustrate well the type of wording which encourages higher levels of response.

- What evidence is there to support the view that sexism is built into the structure of the English language? Argue for and against this hypothesis. If you believe the assertion to be true, does it matter? (English)

- Discuss some movements in the life of the Roman Catholic Church in this century which influenced the work of the Second Vatican Council. (European Studies)

- Individual socio-economic-political systems are said to be exemplified by different types of social stratification and mobility. Analyse, with reference to at least one West and one East European country, how far these different types can be observed in actual practice. (European Studies)

- Durkheim's views about the transition from mechanical to organic solidarity with the growing division of labour could be compared to the views of other authors who have discussed the origins of modern society.   Compare and contrast these views with Polanyi's account of a market economy. (Sociology)

- "By any standards, the insect body must be reckoned the most successful of all the solutions to the problems of living on the surface of the earth." Discuss this statement critically, basing your discussion on evidence. (Zoology)

To answer any of the above questions satisfactorily a student would need to demonstrate the skills which typify each of Bloom's cognitive levels as described above. If, however, a student had prior knowledge that one of these questions was to be used in a formal examination and the student had access to a model answer, it would be possible for that student to commit the answer to memory and reproduce what had been learned by rote.   Doubtless examples of essay questions which test the higher cognitive skills could be found in every discipline, but on the other hand one could also find essay-type examination questions which test only knowledge and comprehension.

6.3.2. Attitude Measures

As will be seen from some of the statements of course aims and objectives which were quoted in Chapter 2, course planners may also be interested in the development of particular attitudes in their students, such as a sense of "responsibility, trustworthiness and confidentiality" and a "sensitivity to the needs of others and concern for other persons" (Engel and Clarke, 1979, p. 71).

It is unfortunate that there is much less written on the measurement of attitudes (for grading purposes) than on knowledge and skills.   There are, of course, many measures of attitudes which are used by psychologists and personnel officers.   Some which are suitable for use in teacher education, such as the Rokeach Dogmatism Scale and the Minnesota Teacher Attitudes Inventory, are described by Peck and Tucker (1973); while Khan and Weiss (1973) discuss some of the more general matters relating to the teaching of attitudes, or as they say, "affective responses", with examples from a number of curriculum areas.   In the same volume as the last two studies, Trent and Cohen (1973) summarise the research on the effects of the teaching environment on attitudes of students and teachers in higher education.   Some of this research is particularly applicable to those institutions which expect their students to develop certain moral values.

As was noted above, affective objectives are particularly important in medical education.   The Medical Faculty at the University of Newcastle, N.S.W. has developed standardised procedures for measuring the extent to which their students are able to demonstrate attitudes which the Faculty deems to be desirable in a medical practitioner. Saunders et al. (1982, p. 154) describe how their measuring scales were developed and give examples.   An understanding by both supervisors and students of reasons why each may hold differing and frequently conflicting viewpoints is important in many areas of higher education, particularly post-graduate studies.   At the undergraduate level the development of acceptable attitudes is an important objective in many professional courses, including theology, teacher education and environmental studies.   Rolph and Rolph (1982) describe a procedure for use in practice teaching which is designed to assist a student teacher's and a supervisor's understanding of their own and each other's perspectives on a lesson being evaluated. This technique could also be used in the training of other professionals. Another example of the assessment of affective objectives is given by Johnstone, Percival and Reid (1981). In a brief report on chemistry teaching in Glasgow University, they refer to students' need to consider controversial employment and environmental issues in relation to decisions about suitable manufacturing processes in industrial chemistry.

In any course where controversial matters are likely to be relevant it is important for teachers to be aware of the possibility that their students may be at different levels of intellectual or ethical development, as described originally by Perry (1970) and outlined in Section 3.2.2 of Chapter 3 of this book. Because students in their earlier years of higher education may not have progressed beyond the the lower levels of development (as defined by Perry), university and college teachers should think seriously about the desirability or otherwise of including measures of students' levels of ethical and intellectual development in any formal system of assessment.

On the one hand it could be argued that it is just as legitimate to include measures of ethical development or value judgments as it is to include measures of students' ability to analyse, apply or evaluate knowledge. On the other hand, it would be claimed that attitudes are matters for personal decision and should not be allowed to influence a student's grades in examinations. On balance, where it is agreed that members of a profession, such as theology, law, medicine or accountancy, should be able to demonstrate specified attitudes or ethical principles, some measure of these should be built into the assessment system.

This need for a greater emphasis on subjective elements in the study of a discipline is propounded by Collier (1984):

> In practice, however, this (higher education) training focusses almost exclusively on the analysis of the objective, factual or conceptual aspects or components of the issue - the economic, for example, and/or the political, the geographical, the historical aspects; it seldom gives any systematic attention to the subjective components in the thinking of the parties to the controversy; very rarely indeed does it give detailed and continuing attention to those components in the thinking of students engaged in probing the issue. In short, the handling of complex issues is too exclusively intellectual, or cognitive, or ratiocinative, and the people emerging from higher education are quite inappropriately prepared to deal with the subjective components which give rise to the controversies that surround such issues. In the contemporary world, however, the potential scale of conflict is so vast, the scope so extensive, the outbreak so contagious, that such exclusively cerebral training in higher education is no longer adequate. (pp. 27-28)

Although Collier advocates teaching approaches which are designed to help students deal with controversial issues, there is no reference in his article to any formal assessment of these qualities in students. He appears to be suggesting that as a result of their experiences students should be capable of judging whether they themselves and their fellow members of project teams have developed an ability to handle controversies satisfactorily; in other words their judgment is based on a combination of self and peer assessment.

6.3.3. Levels of Affective Responses

Krathwohl *et al.* (1964) identify five major levels at which students respond to educational objectives in the affective domain. The description which follows is based on a summary by Bloom, Hastings and Madaus (1971 pp. 273-277). It may be used as a guide to tertiary teachers who wish to compare the levels reached by students at different stages in a course, or indeed within a single lecture or tutorial.

The five levels are:

1. **Receiving**, namely some sign that the student is prepared to learn, as may be indicated by presence at classes. Krathwohl's group note that this basic level of "receiving" may itself become manifest at three sub-levels, namely:

   a. **Awareness** of visual or oral stimuli from the lecturer, without necessarily being able to recall the nature of the stimuli. (Most of us can recognise that this is the highest level reached by at least some of our students in the less exciting parts of our lectures and therefore we seek ways of varying the stimuli in order to raise the level of our students' responses.)

   b. **Willingness to receive** stimuli from the teacher with no attempt being made by the student to avoid the stimuli. (The latter would be indicated when a student masks out the sound of a lecture by engaging in conversation with another student or listening to music through headphones.)

   c. **Controlled or selected attention** occurs when a student shows signs of attending to some stimuli in an environment where there are many. (Students may, for example, only pay attention in a lecture when the overhead projector is used.)

2. **Responding**, i.e. the student displays a minimum level of commitment to the material being taught yet may appear to be gaining some satisfaction from the subject. As with "Awareness", "Responding" may be demonstrated at three sub-levels.

   a. **Acquiescence in responding**, which implies a passive obedience by the student to any instructions from the teacher, such as writing down definitions or examining a specimen in a laboratory.

   b. **Willingness to respond**, which indicates that the student voluntarily obeys instructions, not because the student fears any kind of penalty or reproof.

   c. **Satisfaction in response** occurs when a student appears to derive some satisfaction from his or her voluntary response to the teacher or the instructional materials.

3. **Valuing**, i.e. an appreciation by the student of the worth of pursuing particular educational objectives. As with other major levels, this level may be further subdivided into:

    a. **Acceptance of a Value** as is indicated when a student is prepared to be identified with certain beliefs or points of view;

    b. **Preference for a Value**, which is an intermediate stage between acceptance and commitment, and

    c. **Commitment**, when the belief is expressed in action on the part of the student.

4. **Organization**, i.e. an attempt by the student to arrange a set of values into a hierarchical system so that relationships between different beliefs held by the student become clear. Where there are apparent conflicts, the student identifies which belief is the more important. Two subdivisions of this level have been identified:

    a. **Conceptualization of a Value** when the student can see how one set of values relates to another or how a new attitude or belief fits into the student's previously held set of beliefs, and

    b. **Organization of a Value System** when the student is beginning to develop a philosophy of life which incorporates a "complex of possibly disparate values" which the student attempts to bring into an ordered relationship with one another.

5. **Characterization by a Value or Value Complex**, i.e. the highest level of the affective objectives which is reached when the student consistently behaves in accordance with the set of values which he or she has adopted. There are two sub-levels, namely:

    a. **Generalized Set** which, according to Krathwohl, may be an unconscious cluster of attitudes which guides a student's actions without conscious forethought on the part of the student, and

    b. **Characterization**, at which level the value system has become the student's philosophy of life.

It will be seen from the above descriptions that it is generally possible for teachers to judge the levels of affective objectives being reached by observing their students' behaviour, provided of course that the class is small enough. One of the advantages of the tutorial system in many colleges and universities is that it allows tutors (or teaching assistants) to make the type of close observations required to determine whether students are reaching the desired levels of affective objectives. There is, of course, a fear on the part of some educators that the inclusion of affective objectives in a teaching program can be viewed as indoctrination. This problem is discussed in Chapter 10 of Bloom, Hastings and Madaus (1971, pp. 225-229) in which they refer to dangers of failing to evaluate affective outcomes.

6.3.4. Objectives in the Psychomotor Domain

Psychomotor objectives, or those dealing with manipulative skills, are important in some sections of higher education more than others. They are, of course, most important in many branches of technical and further education - in art, carpentry, hairdressing, music and so on. At the university level their importance is seen more in languages, medical subjects, science, engineering and architecture than in the humanities or social sciences.

Just as methods have to be devised to enable teachers to identify whether their students have reached desired levels of affective objectives, so it is important that teachers in those subjects where psychomotor objectives are relevant should incorporate some measures of students' psychomotor skills in the assessment scheme. Because the types of skills differ so widely from one discipline to another, it would not be useful to describe possible approaches here.

Simpson (1966) identifies five levels of psychomotor objectives, brief definitions of which are given below:

1. **Perception**, i.e. sensing, usually by sight, hearing or touch, a need for or the possibility of some sequence of mechanical operations;

2. **Set**, i.e. a readiness on the part of the student for a particular kind of action;

3. **Guided Response**, i.e. an action or series of actions by the student under the direct guidance of the teacher;

4. **Mechanism**, i.e. the stage reached when a learned response has become habitual, and

5. **Complex Response**, i.e. the level at which a student can perform a complex series of actions smoothly and efficiently.

6.3.5. Skills in the Science Laboratory

Laboratory exercises in higher education may serve many different purposes. Some of the reasons for making laboratory work compulsory were listed in the previous chapter. It is the course designer's responsibility to decide which of the many possible reasons are important enough to carry weight in examinations and, if so, what that weight should be. An example from the biological sciences will illustrate what is meant.

In their first year classes at university or college, students normally learn to use a microscope; they may be taught how to cut sections of tissues and prepare the sections for microsocopic examination and they are usually expected to be able to recognise different parts of a tissue. In their theoretical work, if not in the laboratory classes the students are also expected to demonstrate that they know how the various tissues function in an organism; there may be links between anatomy or histology on the one hand and physiology or biochemistry on the other. In some cases there will be links with ecological studies or evolution. Which of all these topics is to be examined and in what context?

Apart from their ability to use particular scientific instruments, such as microscopes, spectrometers and balances, successful science students are expected to be able to select the equipment and technique or sequence of operations needed for solving each problem. The teacher must judge whether each of these skills is important enough to warrant its inclusion in a formal practical examination. For each skill which is being examined the teacher has also to decide how much time is to be allocated for testing it and the proportion of marks which should be allowed for successful demonstration of that skill.

6.3.6. Listening and Speaking Skills in Foreign Languages

While foreign language courses have many features in common with English Literature and History, they are distinctive in that an important aim for most students is to acquire the ability to understand the spoken language and to speak fluently, particularly if the student wishes to use that language for communication with native speakers. For example, it is becoming increasingly popular for students to study Economics or Commerce and a foreign language, especially Japanese, concurrently. For such a student the study of Japanese literature may appear to be irrelevant, yet many language teachers, particularly in universities, have specialised in the study of literature and believe that students are best introduced to a language through the study of its literature. The needs of students who are studying a language for use in commerce or some similar reason should not be overlooked. These students must develop skills in listening and speaking in addition to their knowledge of vocabulary, grammar, literature and the culture of the country.

Valette (1967) describes a number of simple tests for discrimination, retention and comprehension in listening, and although her book is designed mainly for secondary teachers, the principles she enunciates may be applied at the tertiary level if more suitable examples are chosen. In describing these tests, Valette mentions the need for discrimination of phonemes, recognition of intonation patterns where they exist, and ability to hear and distinguish accented syllables and stressed words. She also suggests that testing of speaking skills is made simpler and thus becomes more reliable if the tester concentrates on certain features of the student's speech, ignoring others for the duration of the test. Obviously decisions about what will be marked and what will be ignored must be made before the test is given, and in this case students would not be told exactly which features of their speech will be marked, only that the teacher will be concentrating on some features of the student's speech and ignoring others for the purpose of this test.

6.4. TEST DESIGN

From the foregoing sections on types and levels of educational objectives it should be clear that the task of designing a test or examination is not something that can be left to the last minute. Even tutorial exercises require considerable thought to ensure that students demonstrate the levels of knowledge, skills and attitudes which can be reasonably expected at that stage of the course, and that over a period of time the range of skills and topics is fully explored.

The task is even more demanding when final examinations are being set. If there have been other measures of students' ability at regular stages throughout the course it is not necessary for the final examination to test every part of the course or the attainment of every objective. In any case, time would not permit this. Nevertheless when a final examination is a normal part of the assessment procedure, it is desirable that the examination should test a representative selection from the course. The use of a grid similar to the one in Table 6.1 will help to ensure not only that the examination draws on a reasonable sample of topics and levels of understanding, but that the types of questions are sufficiently varied to make the paper interesting and challenging. The use of different question formats will also lessen the chances of certain students being unduly advantaged or disadvantaged because they are good at one type of question such as essay writing, drawing or selecting the correct response from a multiple-choice question.

Advice on the construction of multiple-choice questions is available in many more specialised publications, examples of which include Cockburn and Ross (1977i), Educational Testing Service (1963) and Clift and Imrie (1981, pp. 73-86). The main points to remember are:

- avoid ambiguities;

- ensure that alternative choices (distracters) all appear reasonably plausible or that they represent the types of error which are frequently made by students;

- the correct response should be about the same length as the distracters in order to avoid giving unnecessary clues.

6.5. ASSESSING GROUP WORK

6.5.1. Contributions to Discussions

Tutorial discussions form an integral part of many teaching programs, perhaps more so in the humanities and social sciences than in languages, mathematics or the natural sciences, although even in these fields discussions of student problems and controversial issues are becoming more prevalent. If students are expected to learn from these discussions, it would be natural to assess in some way their contributions to the tutorials. The problem is, of course, how to measure the quality, as opposed to the quantity of student contributions. The easiest method is to ask each student to take responsibility for presenting a brief paper or leading the discussion at one of the tutorial sessions, but experience has shown that such methods have most value for the student whose turn it is, but very little value for others in the class.

Some lecturers overcome this problem by making attendance at tutorials more or less compulsory (i.e. students are not allowed to sit for the final examination if they have missed more than say two tutorials without a good excuse). Apart from this rather negative approach, the lecturer may award some marks which are determined by the quality of brief notes on the topic for the day which are submitted each week by all students. A further mark may be awarded on the basis of contribution to the group discussion. assessed subjectively by the lecturer or even by the students themselves.

6.5.2. Syndicates

An interesting and more rewarding alternative to the presentation of papers from individual students at tutorials, is for three or four students to form a syndicate which takes responsibility for the whole tutorial, or as is more likely, a seminar. From time to time syndicate work is also used for preparing major reports which form the main item for assessment in a course. The individual members of the syndicate take responsibility for different aspects of the task, such as reviewing the literature, designing the research project, collecting and analysing data, writing the report and presenting their findings to the class, sometimes using audiovisual materials prepared by a member of the team.   In some of these group activities it is a relatively simple matter to determine the extent to which each member of the syndicate has contributed to the total assignment, and grades can be allocated accordingly.   It is more common, however, for a single report to be presented, sometimes by one member of the team, and the lecturer has no easy way of deciding the proportion of the total mark to be awarded to each group member.

The simplest solution to this dilemma is for the teacher to award a mark or grade for the total project, using similar criteria to those which are followed in marking a major essay, a term paper or a thesis.   The grade given for the total project then becomes the grade for each contributor, regardless of the amount of work each has put into the project.   Such a procedure is likely to be unfair to some students, the very good and the very bad, so that if it is thought to be the only workable scheme, students should be told at the beginning of the project and allowed to select their other team members.   A more complex procedure is to ask members of each group to allocate what they regard to be a fair proportion of the total mark to each group member. While most groups will opt for the easy way out and share the marks equally, there will be a significant number of groups in which it will be recognised that some members have contributed much more (or less) than others and should have the marks allocated appropriately.   The teacher can often help groups to determine the criteria which will be used for allocating marks in proportion to the quality of work done.

A third solution is possible where classes are sufficiently small. As before, a total mark is awarded for the project as a whole, but the allocation of grades to individual members of the team is made by the lecturer after each student has been given a "viva" during which the student's general knowledge of the topic is tested and his or her contribution to the team effort is assessed.

6.6. ESSAY MARKING

Many readers will be familiar with an oft-quoted study by Hartog and Rhodes (1935) which demonstrated markers' inability to give the same mark when assessing the same essay a year later, and with a similar study by Dunstan (1959) which found a lack of agreement within a team of markers when each was marking the same essay.   It is unfortunate that these studies have received such wide publicity, as they have tended to bring essays into disrepute in some quarters.

More recent research by Britton et al. (1970) and Gosschalk et al. (1966) claims that the most reliable grading of essays occurs when, prior to marking, lecturers spend time discussing with their colleagues criteria which are likely to influence their judgments, but they do not attempt to attach a weighting to each criterion.   They then read each student's essay and award a mark based on their total impression.

In discussing the marking of essays, Cockburn and Ross (1977h, p. 36) suggest a series of criteria which may be used when determining the grade to be awarded.   They acknowledge that for different subjects and marking schemes new lists of criteria would need to be prepared, nevertheless their list, which is reproduced in Table 6.2, may be of assistance to those with little experience in marking essays.   When a list of criteria, such as the one prepared by Cockburn and Ross, has been prepared, it is most important that it be made available to students when essay topics or assignments are set.   If there is a study skills centre within the institution, it is a good idea to provide

Study Skills counsellors with criterion lists.

TABLE 6.2

GRADE	DESCRIPTION
A+/A	Excellent critical and conceptual analysis; comprehensive survey of relevant issues; well argued; well presented; relevant reading effectively incorporated.
A-/B+/B	Good critical and conceptual analysis; good survey of relevant issues; satisfactory presentation; relevant reading effectively incoporated.
B-/C+/C	Rather more descriptive than critical and conceptual ;analysis lacks clarity in parts; evidence of relevant reading but not always effectively used.
C-/D+	Perfunctory; largely descriptive; disorganised and lacking in detail.
D/D-	Perfunctory; almost entirely descriptive; narrow in conception; poorly argued.
E	No evidence of understanding; little evidence of a serious attempt.
O	Not presented.

Beard (1976, pp. 191-192) lists seventeen factors which might be taken into account in the marking of essays, and although the list was originally prepared for teachers of English, most could be used in marking essays in other subjects. Edited examples from her list are reproduced below.

TABLE 6.3

Qualities of a Successful Essay

1. Evidence that the question has been read thoroughly;

2. Clear listing of main points in a logical order;

3. Concise arguments;

4. References and quotations used in context and either cited correctly or, if

paraphrased, this would be acknowledged;

5. Generalisations based only on suitable evidence;

6. Written within the framework of the subject, e.g. literary criticism rather than history or philosophy.

Wherever possible students should be told how their essays will be marked, and generally speaking, students have a right to know afterwards the basis on which their marks were awarded. There may be occasions when a lecturer will wish to make the essay topic deliberately open in order to test students' ability to interpret what information is needed and how it would best be presented. Even when encouragement of creativity is the lecturer's purpose it is desirable for the students to be informed.

6.6.1. Helpful Comments

Lecturers are often criticised for failing to provide sufficient feedback on the quality of a student's work or the level of attainment reached by the student. "Simple" marks such as 7 out of 10, or β ++, or equally "simple" comments such as "Good Work" or "You could do better than this", do not really tell students much about how their work compares with other members of the class, whether it comes up to the teacher's expectations or, most important of all, what the students need to do to improve their levels of performance.

If the class is small enough and there are not too many essays to be marked at the one time it is possible for the teacher to write quite specific comments and suggestions on each student's essay and to arrange for each student to receive his or her marked essay at an interview session in the teacher's office. There are times, however, when such a practice would be ill-advised, particularly if there is any possibility of a charge of sexual harassment against the teacher.

With larger classes an alternative procedure to individual comments and interviews has to be adopted. One practice which I have found to be quite successful is to give each student a mark or grade for the essay, write a small number of comments which apply only to a particular student's essay, and provide for the class a set of notes which describe the criteria used in determining grades, a listing of common errors and suggestions for acceptable approaches to the essay topic(s) which had been set. If the class agrees, it is also very helpful to have one or two of the better essays photocopied and distributed to members of the class, particularly if there is more than one satisfactory approach to the assignment.

6.7. REDEEMABILITY AND PROGRESSIVE ASSESSMENT

Instead of every piece of work contributing directly to their final grades, students should be encouraged to submit tentative answers to problems or drafts of essays, particularly when they are exploring new topics or developing new skills. At times the degree of difficulty of the work is such that only the teachers or other academics are able to give assistance. However there are many occasions when students can help each other, possibly by meeting together in the absence of a teacher to discuss one another's drafts. Although such a practice is obviously open to abuse, students who have developed a good rapport among themselves and with their teacher can learn a great deal from one another.

The main advantages of any system of redeemability is that it encourages students to reach their full potential and does not penalise them for relatively minor errors of judgment.   It follows that the increase in workloads for both staff and students could well be disproportionate to the value gained from extra work on the same topic and thus prove to be a disadvantage.

6.8. THE FINAL GRADE

At the end of each course it is the teacher's responsibility to let students know how successful they were in achieving the objectives of the course and to submit to the institution a list showing either marks or grades for all enrolled students, and sometimes an order of merit listing.   If these results are based on students' performance in one examination the determination of marks, grades and orders of merit is much easier than when assessment has been spread throughout the year, or even throughout a whole professional degree program.

6.8.1. Combining Marks and Preparing Orders of Merit Lists

Much has been written on the problems of combining marks from quite different types of work to produce an overall final grade. For example, Dunn (1967) shows that the practice of adding raw scores (e.g. $40/60 + 18/20 + 5/10 + 7/10 = 70/100$) can be quite misleading and under some circumstances produce orders of merit which do not reflect the grades which would be expected if they were based on a teacher's judgment of the general quality of a student's work.   This is particularly likely to happen if a very small range of marks is allocated for the major project - in the above case out of 60.   An amusing paper entitled "The First Shall be Last", the origin of which I have been unable to trace. gives a fictitious account of a group of students whose order of merit was completely reversed when their marks were adjusted in an effort to overcome the effects of faulty weighting.

Nisbet and Entwistle (1970, pp. 92-95) demonstrate how subjects (or individual components of the assessment scheme) for which a relatively wide range of marks has been awarded, will carry much greater weight in determining the order of merit of students than a subject or assignment in which the range of marks has been small.   To take an extreme and rather simplistic example, a lecturer may decide that the assessment for a course will have one major and one minor component.   The major component, a research project, may carry 80% of the marks and the minor component. a multiple-choice test, 20%. If, however, the range of marks for the research project is from sixty to sixty-five out of a possible eighty while the marks in the test are distributed between zero to twenty, a student who had the highest score in the field study but whose performance in the multiple-choice test had been poor could well be ranked near or at the bottom of the class.

Various methods have been proposed for dealing with problems such as the one just described.   If there is any danger of students being unfairly treated as a result of some components of the assessment scheme having a wider spread of marks than others, the best procedure is to convert the "raw scores" to "standard scores".   Procedures for doing this are relatively simple with modern calculators which have statistical functions, particularly a capability for calculating the mean and standard deviation.   They are even easier if the teacher has access to a computer.   Details of the statistical procedures are available in most books on assessment, including Ferguson (1966, p. 255) and

Tuckman (1975, p. 491). Once the mean and standard deviation have been determined for all scores in any set, the raw scores can be transformed by a simple formula which sets the same predetermined mean and standard deviation for each set of scores.

If the teacher wishes the standardised scores to have a mean of 50 and a standard deviation of 15, the following formula would be used:

$$\text{Standard Score} = 50 + 15(\text{Raw Score - Mean})/\text{Standard Deviation}$$

Once the raw scores have been transformed into standardised scores one can safely add the marks for different components of an examination, applying weightings as desired to match the importance of each component.

6.8.2. The Dubious Value of Merit Lists

Because the assessment process is dependent on so many different factors ranging from the teacher's selection of assessment procedures, essay topics and exercises to subjective judgments about the quality of answers, great care should be taken when establishing an order of merit list. It should be clear that any order of merit list in which prize winners (or failing students) are separated from others by only a mark or two is quite suspect. Examiners then have to consider other evidence which might separate one student from another. Difficulties in making such judgments have led some institutions to abandon the publication of orders of merit. Even so, the allocation of grades such as High Distinction, Distinction, Credit, Pass, Conditional Pass and Fail, or A, B, C, D, and F is a type of ranking which most institutions prefer to retain, as the grades are claimed to be indicators of levels of achievement.

6.8.3. A Comprehensive Final Year Assessment

One of the responsibilities of a professional faculty is to judge whether its graduates are capable of undertaking the range of tasks expected in a newly appointed member of that profession. In many cases a judgment such as this is made on the basis of a student's performance in examinations and field placements over the years, but this assumes that knowledge or skills exhibited by the student in the earlier years of a degree program are present to the same extent on graduation. If a suitable form of final assessment can be adopted, more accurate assumptions about a new graduate's potential could be made by the institution awarding the qualification, the graduating student, the profession as a whole or likely employers.

A comprehensive approach to the assessment of final year medical students which has been adopted by the University of Newcastle, New South Wales, is described by Feletti et al. (1983). They describe how students' achievement of the stated objectives for the whole degree program are assessed at various stages during the final year and suitable weightings are assigned to each piece of work. The assessment instruments used include ratings by clinical supervisors, various types of tests and essays, and an evaluation of a student's interview of a simulated patient. The authors report that this system of summative assessment is well received by students, assessors and program evaluators.

6.9. THE PLACE OF ASSESSMENT IN A COURSE PLAN

Teaching, learning and assessment are closely related. Although this chapter has been placed near the end of the book, and usually the most important part of assessment comes near the end of a course, it is important to reiterate the need for course planners to think about the type and placement of all forms of assessment. This should take place before the course begins and any necessary modifications to the plans for assessment would be made later in the light of knowledge gained from progress tests and other assignments.

7. EVALUATING THE COURSE

The task of planning a unit of instruction is far from complete when the teacher has determined the objectives, selected and put into order the content, chosen or prepared suitable reading material and designed the methods of assessment. Even when the first group of students has completed the course there still remains a need for evaluating the effectiveness of the course in order that judgments can be made about future versions of that course. Thus, an essential part of course design is planning for regular evaluations of the course. Much of this chapter is based on the work of staff in the Office for Research in Academic Methods (ORAM) at the Australian National University. A fuller description of their work is available in Miller (1984). In the present chapter some general principles of evaluation will be discussed and various approaches to this technique will be suggested. For a more comprehensive treatment of evaluation procedures the reader is urged to consult Roe and McDonald's *Informed Professional Judgement* (1983).

7.1. EVALUATION DEFINED

As used in the present context, an evaluation of a course implies a systematic examination of all aspects of the course: its prerequisites and place in the total curriculum, the selection and ordering of content, the choice of teaching and assessment methods, and the destination of graduates. It is usually undertaken with a view to improving the course for future cohorts of students, but other reasons for evaluations will also be considered.

Evaluation should be distinguished from "assessment", which is a measure of students' progress or achievement, and "accountability", which is a public recognition of the worth of a course or, more frequently, of the total curriculum (Lacey and Lawton, 1981; McCormick, 1982).

7.2. REASONS FOR COURSE EVALUATIONS

At least seven reasons why university teachers may wish to evaluate their courses have been identified. Experience in the Australian National University has shown that evaluations are likely to be more effective and more acceptable to students and teachers if the reasons for the particular evaluation have been clarified before the evaluation begins.

7.2.1. Investigating a Known Problem

One of the most common problems leading to a request for an evaluation is that present wastage or failure rates may be much higher than in previous years or in courses thought to be at a similar level of difficulty. Another area of difficulty may be excessive workloads. While there may be simple explanations for each of these situations, such as the teacher having quite unreasonable expectations of students, it is more likely that the problem has a number of causes, examples of which are lack of clarity regarding assessment requirements, uncertainty about students' background knowledge or the teacher's failure to refer students to appropriate sections of the text.

7.2.2. Improving an Existing Program

There are times when a course has been taught for some years without any major change and students appear to be reasonably satisfied with what is being taught, yet the teacher feels that some changes are needed, if only to provide fresh motivation for the teacher. In these circumstances it is important for the teacher to ascertain whether there are any features of the program which students would like changed and which features the students deem to be most valuable. The evaluation may focus on student satisfaction with the text, the arrangements for tutorials or laboratory classes, or the choice and arrangement of topics.

7.2.3. Examining the Impact of an Innovation

Whenever major changes have been made in course content or methods of teaching it is important to ascertain the impact of the innovation on student motivation and learning. Sometimes an innovation, such as the use of computers in teaching, may be introduced as a result of one person's enthusiasm, in which case it is important to be able to evaluate the effect of the innovation on the students. For example, recent studies at Carnegie-Mellon University by Kiesler, Siegel and McGuire (1984) have shown that when students in that university were encouraged to purchase computers at a substantial discount and use them in the majority of courses, a number of important changes occurred in the nature of their interaction with teachers and with other students. The researchers found that computer-mediated groups took longer to reach a consensus than did face-to-face groups and there is a suggestion that decisions might have been different if discussions had been face-to-face (*ibid* pp. 1128-1129).

7.2.4. Reorganisation Within a Program

From time to time both teachers and students agree that the content of a course is both interesting and essential for any further understanding of the subject, yet students are experiencing problems because the order in which topics are introduced does not appear logical to them. Sometimes a new topic is introduced in a lecture when it would have been more appropriately introduced in a discussion group, on a field trip or in a laboratory exercise. An evaluation which focusses on course objectives and the order and manner in which new topics are presented, can help identify and overcome such problems.

7.2.5. Validation of a Program or a Curriculum

Earlier in this chapter the distinction was made between "evaluation" and "accountability". "Validation" is normally more closely linked with accountability as it implies that some seal of public or professional approval has been given to a particular curriculum or to a course which forms part of that curriculum. In many cases the validation is based on an examination of published objectives, course outlines and laboratory manuals, examination papers or essay topics, and, in some cases, samples of students' answers to exam questions and other assignments. It is rare for validations of this type to include the type of detailed evaluation which is described in the present chapter, yet where the results of student surveys are available they can be quite helpful to accreditation panels, perhaps by pointing to areas of duplication within a course or between two related courses or by indicating a need for changing the recommended textbook.

7.2.6. Assisting Students in Selection of Courses

In many institutions the student association produces an "Alternative Handbook" which is designed to advise prospective students in their selection of courses and sometimes teachers. Information in these handbooks is said to be based on student reactions to each course or teacher as revealed in surveys undertaken by the student association. Unless response rates are reasonably high, there is a danger that the information and advice contained in the alternative handbook will not represent the views of most students in a course. There have been cases of alternative handbooks in which descriptions of courses or academic departments are written by one or two students who are very critical. An unfortunate effect of publishing biased reports is that all evaluations of courses by students tend to be devalued and perfectly reasonable recommendations or requests for change are rejected.

7.2.7. Supporting Applications for Tenure or Promotion

Now that proficiency in teaching is being recognised as important for the granting of tenure or promotion, academic staffing committees are looking for means by which teaching proficiency may be judged. At the worst, this is judged by hearsay evidence, as there are few university or college teachers whose teaching is open to public scrutiny. Although the present chapter deals mainly with the evaluations of **courses**, most of the principles enunciated here may be applied to the evaluation of **teaching** or even **teachers**. It is common for course evaluations to incorporate some evaluation of the quality of teaching, yet these are not really suitable for inclusion as evidence in an application for tenure or promotion. The problem is that much of the information obtained from a course evaluation has no relevance to the quality of an individual teacher's work as the course may have been designed completely by another person. Thus an evaluation for tenure or promotion needs to focus on the teaching and only those other aspects of course organisation which are under direct control of the teacher whose performance is being judged.

7.3. SOURCES OF DATA

The type of data sought as a basis for evaluative judgments will be largely determined by the prime reasons for the evaluation. Thus in some cases the views of students about the quality of teaching will be an essential part of the evaluation whereas on other occasions, the evaluation **might** be carried out without reference to current students in the course or program.

7.3.1. Course Descriptions

Whether the evaluation is being conducted as part of an accreditation exercise or for the improvement of teaching and learning, an examination by the evaluator of formal statements about prerequisites, objectives, content, required reading and assessment should be undertaken almost at the beginning of the evaluation. The purpose of such an examination would be to indicate to the evaluator the type of materials made available to students and to suggest whether some measure of student satisfaction with these course documents is likely to be required.

7.3.2. Course Co-ordinator

Any evaluation which does not take into consideration the views of the course co-ordinator will omit essential information about the course. It is therefore desirable that course co-ordinators attempt to answer a few key questions about the course at the end of each semester or year. One could use the questions which were asked at the beginning of this book, or the slightly more focussed checklist from Table 7.1.

TABLE 7.1

Checklist for Evaluating One's Own Course

Goals What were the three most important things I expected my students to gain from this course?

Objectives In order to achieve the goals for this course, what did my students have to do by the end of the course?

Learning How and where did I expect my students to develop each of the skills or attitudes listed among my objectives (e.g. from lectures, discussions, reading and/or assignments, practice in the laboratory or field work)?

Prerequisites What knowledge or skills did I expect in my students when they enrolled for this course?

Content and Objectives
As I critically consider the range of content which I expected students to cover in this course, can I see why each item was necessary for attaining the knowledge and skills which I listed in answer to the previous question?

Content and Expectations
If this course was a pre-requisite for another course, or part of a curriculum leading to a professional qualification, am I satisfied that the objectives and content matched the expectations of teachers in later courses and the needs of the profession?

References Did I give my students sufficient guidance in the use of texts and references; were the materials readily available, and was the recommended reading the most suitable for achieving the objectives of the course?

Key Principles How were my students expected to distinguish the key principles within the mass of content?

Links   Did I provide sufficient opportunities for my students to seek links between the content of this course and related material in cognate disciplines, their prior experiences and their future careers?

Assessment   Am I satisfied that the system of assessment which was used in this course was an adequate indication of each student's progress towards the goals which I identified in answer to the first question on this checklist, and did the various tests, exercises and essays measure students' native ability or their learning in **this** course? (from Miller, 1984)

7.3.3. Current and Former Students

Most evaluations within the Australian National University depend heavily on information obtained from students currently enrolled in or just completing the course being evaluated. The reliability and validity of student ratings have been discussed in detail elsewhere (e.g. Doyle and Crichton, 1978; Braskamp, 1980). Experience at the ANU has shown that initial objections to the use of student evaluators are overcome if the questionnaire gathers information sought by the teacher. Examples of information which is useful will be given later in the chapter.

A frequently raised objection to the use of student data is that students may not be aware of the value of a course until later in their studies or after they begin their professional careers. This criticism has some validity when applied to service courses such as statistics or chemistry or to courses which are required by outside organisations as essential for recognition of a professional qualification. In order to counter this objection it is helpful to question recent graduates or senior students. There is, of course, a danger of errors of interpretation resulting from biased sampling. The possibility of such a bias is signalled when the distribution of certain categories among the responding population differs significantly from that of the original population of students in the course being evaluated. For example, when a fairly large proportion of part-time students had been enrolled, yet only a few part-time students responded to the survey, one would have reason to question the validity of the findings, particularly if there were any evidence to show that the two categories of students were likely to respond differently on some items in the questionnaire.

7.3.4. Professional Evaluators

In institutions which have academic development units (or centres for the improvement of teaching) it is possible for university teachers to request advice on teaching and on course design from a member of the unit with expertise in theory and practice of university teaching. The objective approach of such an observer more than compensates for any lack of familiarity with the subject matter.

7.4. TYPES OF DATA

Views on course structure and teaching from a professional evaluator, who rarely sees more than a small proportion of classes in the subject being evaluated will naturally vary in quality from the information which is available from students. This section will focus on the latter, which is mainly gathered by means of questionnaires, but could be obtained by structured interviews.

7.4.1. Respondents' Backgrounds

In any formal evaluation using data from students it is usual to gather some background information about respondents, even though the identity of individual respondents is not generally sought. Demographic data and information about students' backgrounds may be used to indicate whether certain categories of students (as defined by age, sex, previous studies or work experiences) respond differently to other students.

7.4.2. Reactions to Course Content

The most helpful reactions will be ones which identify those sections of the course which are causing students the greatest difficulty, or which students judge to be a waste of time as they have already studied the material elsewhere. Interpretations of these data should take into account information about respondents (as described in the previous section), in the first instance by means of cross-tabulations, but with the significance of any differences determined by appropriate statistical tests.

As was mentioned earlier in Chapter 4, university and college teachers need to make assumptions about levels of background knowledge brought by students to first year classes. These assumptions are even more difficult to make when students come from secondary schools which offer a broad range of courses to students in their final years. Students with different secondary backgrounds, or with different career expectations, are likely to evaluate course content in quite distinctive ways and it may be necessary for teachers to take these differences into consideration when planning a course. (See also Miller, 1980, pp. 85-88)

7.4.3. Use of Course Materials

From the teacher's point of view a textbook may be ideal in that it covers all the material for the course in approximately the desired order and pitched at the right level of difficulty. The tables and illustrations may be clear, yet students may not be using the book! The teacher would therefore be seeking reasons for this lack of use by students. Do they have too much reading to do and are they unaware of the relative value of the different publications on their reading lists or is the recommended text too expensive for the average student to purchase?

7.4.4. Suitability of Teaching Methods

It is generally acknowledged that professional evaluators or educational technologists are in a better position than students to make informed judgments on the suitability of different teaching methods. Two reasons for this assumption are that students would have experienced a more limited range of methods in their tertiary studies and they may be tempted to confuse a teacher's popularity with good teaching. Even so, it is possible that methods which are suggested by educational technologists lack appeal for the students, or are too difficult for some teachers to implement. It is therefore important for teachers to obtain the views of students **and** educational technologists on the suitability of teaching methods to ascertain whether any change is desired. It is certainly not good enough for a teacher to continue teaching a course in traditional ways when more efficient methods are available.

7.4.5. Suitability of Assessment Procedures

The whole issue of assessment is too large for any detailed treatment in the present book, and some aspects of the subject were dealt with in the previous chapter. In that chapter no mention was made of the important concepts of **validity** and **reliability** which are described in more detail elsewhere (e.g. Satterly, 1981; Mehrens and Lehmann, 1973). For our present purposes "Validity" may be defined as the ability of a test (or other form of assessment) to measure what it claims to be measuring and "reliability" as the ability of a test to give consistent scores for similar performances.

While it would be desirable for all course evaluations to incorporate methods for measuring the validity and reliability of any assessment used. it is not possible to do this through questionnaires to students. What can be learned from student responses is whether they think the assessment system is fair, whether assessment tasks match the stated objectives for the course and whether students are given adequate feedback on their performance, particularly at earlier stages in the program.

7.4.6. Distribution of Workloads

Attempts to estimate the number of hours worked per week by students on course-related tasks have generally been unsuccessful, due to the fact that the workload for any one student varies considerably throughout the year. and even for a group of students enrolled in the same programs with the same assignments there will be considerable variation in the amount of time spent. It is nevertheless helpful for teaching staff to be made aware of workload problems created or exacerbated by unavailability of prescribed reading materials. difficulties in consulting tutors, or clashes in deadlines for assignments.

7.5. METHODS OF GATHERING DATA

The method chosen for gathering data for an evaluation will largely be determined by the purpose of the evaluation. In this section three methods will be described, namely subjective judgments, student achievements and surveys of student opinion.

7.5.1. Subjective Judgments

A subjective consideration of one's own teaching and course design is an important, if not essential, part of any evaluation. Use of a checklist similar to the one given earlier in this chapter will provide some direction to the teacher, but an even more helpful procedure is for a colleague to interview the teacher, preferably after the colleague has attended one or more classes and examined the course materials. The purpose of the interview is more to help the teacher focus on different aspects of the course than to express a professional judgment on the course, although the colleague's views could be quite informative.

7.5.2. Measures of Student Achievement

Much of the earlier research comparing different teaching methods was influenced by experimental designs which had proved so effective in agriculture and medicine. Attempts were made to demonstrate the superiority of one method over another by comparing students' performance before and after being taught in either an "experimental" or a "control" group. Problems with this type of research were recognised by McKeachie (1963) over two decades ago and more recently by Trent and Cohen (1973), Verma and Beard (1981) and Bassey (1981), to name but a few.

Whereas in Agriculture and, to a lesser extent, Medicine it is possible to vary only one factor at a time (say the pH of the soil), any attempt to vary one factor in teaching (particularly in Higher Education) invariably influences other factors. As a result, attempts to compare teaching methods (or courses) by noting differences in student performance either led to contradictory results or to the conclusion that there was "no statistical difference between the groups". Reasons for the apparent failure of achievement tests to reflect differences in the quality of teaching are not difficult to find. For example, "poor" teaching may stimulate students to work harder or one teacher may prepare students better for the final test without necessarily teaching as well as another teacher.

Just as it could be quite misleading to use tests of student performance as a direct measure of the effectiveness of teaching, it is equally dangerous to judge the success of a course by the achievement of its past students. Nevertheless in any broad evaluation of individual courses and of total curricula, it would be unwise to overlook any information which is available from pass, failure and withdrawal rates or the relevance of their study to the careers of graduates.

7.5.3. Surveys of Student Opinion

Within the Australian National University (ANU), the Office for Research in Academic Methods (ORAM) makes extensive use of student surveys in the evaluation of courses and teaching (Miller, 1984). Brief reference was made earlier in this chapter to the rationale for placing considerable dependence on student opinion in evaluating and possibly modifying teaching programs. Use of student evaluations has also been argued many times in the literature, recent examples being by Doyle (1983) and by Roe and McDonald (1983). Although interviews can provide a wealth of information, they are time-consuming, both for gathering information and for analysing the results. If, however, classes are small, a series of interviews, either of each student separately or of groups of two or three students at a time, can be most rewarding. Interviews have been used from time at the ANU, but with a relatively small ORAM staff and a large number of courses to be evaluated, it has been more efficient to gather information by means of questionnaires.

An earlier section of this chapter described the types of information sought from students when courses or teaching are being evaluated. Much of this information can be gathered by means of standardised questions such as those which have been used for many years in universities and colleges in the United States. Standardised questionnaires normally consist of a short series of questions, usually occupying no more than a single sheet of paper, to each of which the student responds by selecting the appropriate box. Responses can then be easily quantified and compared. Examples of these are included in Eble (1970, pp. 98-100), Flood Page (1974, pp. 12-22), Doyle (1983, pp. 142-146), Miller (1984, p. 14), Roe and McDonald (1983, pp. 88-101, 169-175) and Centra (1979, pp. 20-23, 128-129).

Sometimes a standardised questionnaire is prepared, distributed and analysed by a group of students for use in a "Counter Course Handbook"; in other cases, particularly the United States, distribution and analysis of the questionnaire is the responsibility of the central administration, sometimes through an Office for Institutional Research. One great advantage of some standardised questionnaires is that they can be analysed directly by computer, thus making results available to teachers or other interested parties within twenty-four hours. There are, however, fewer opportunities in a standardised questionnaire for including questions on specific features in a course or for students to make written (and often more perceptive) comments on aspects of the course.

At the opposite end of the spectrum from standardised questionnaires is the "tailor-made" type of questionnaire which is designed for use in a particular course to provide information on a limited range of problems. Although very successful in pinpointing problem areas and suggesting changes in course structure or teaching, their development is time-consuming and, in many cases, the final form of questions used is identical to that used in standardised questionnaires. For these reasons some academic development units have moved towards what might be termed a "supermarket" or "smorgasbord" approach to questionnaire design.

In the Office for Research in Academic Methods at the Australian National University a computer file has been established containing many different types of questionnaires which can be used in surveys of student opinion. Given the right kind of computer and on-line printer, it is a relatively simple task to develop and print a questionnaire which meets the needs of a particular client. A system similar to this has been operating for some years in the *Service de Pédagogie Universitaire* of the *Université Laval*. Québec (Dufresne, 1978). With the help of a staff member from the *Service*, a teacher requesting a course evaluation selects the items which are most suited to the teacher's needs.

7.5.4. Closed or Open Questions

If the evaluator wishes to have some quantitative measure of student responses to an item, it is usual to use questions to which students respond by selecting (usually) one answer from a number of possible responses. These are much easier to code and therefore less likely to contain errors. The numerical scores thus obtained may be converted to percentages of responses and, if the sample of respondents is both representative and large enough, mean ratings may be easily calculated. Several examples of fixed-choice questions from ORAM evaluations are given in Table 7.2. Other examples are available in the literature, references to which were given earlier in this chapter.

TABLE 7.2

Examples of Fixed-Choice Questions

* Were the objectives made clear to you at the beginning of this unit?

Very clear [ ]   Quite clear [ ]   Not very clear [ ]
Not at all clear [ ]

* At present the law course is made up of a number of compulsory and elective units. Please indicate which (if any) of the compulsory units should be made compulsory and use the following code to signify your main reasons (up to two) for recommending the change.

This unit should be an elective because:-

1 = all units should be elective;
2 = it does not fit into my career plans;
3 = I am not interested in the content;
4 = the material in the unit could be self-taught;
5 = it is not necessary for a basic understanding of the legal system.

* How would you rate the workload for this unit?
Much too heavy [ ]   A little too heavy   [ ]
About right   [ ]   A little too light   [ ]
                        Far too light   [ ]

* If you consider the workload "a little too heavy" or "much too heavy", please indicate which of the following factors contributed to the excessive workload (you may tick more than one box if you wish).

The **amount** of material covered   [ ]
The **difficulty** of the material   [ ]
A lack of structure to the material   [ ]
Uncertainty as to what is required   [ ]
The number of contact hours required   [ ]
The amount of written work required   [ ]
The amount of reading required   [ ]
Other (please specify) ....

There is a fairly obvious weakness with the multiple-choice responses described above. Many students find that none of the choices really matches their interpretation of the situation, so they react by writing in the margin or by tearing up the questionnaire! It is therefore necessary, both from the point of view of obtaining higher response rates, and, because we are interested in what students have to say, to include in every questionnaire a number of "open-ended" questions. Responses to these normally take longer to read, analyse and include in a report, but they add meat to the bones of frequency counts. The two following questions are commonly used at or near the end of an otherwise tightly structured questionnaire:

* Name one or more features of this course or its organisation
  which, in your opinion, were its best features and which
  should be retained in the future.

  ....

  ....

  ....

* Are there any features of this course or its organisation
  which, in your opinion, were its worst features and which
  should be changed or omitted from future courses of this
  type. If so, list them here.

  ....

  ....

  ....

It is, of course, possible to combine features of both types of questions by including within a multiple-choice question an opportunity for students to write comments or explanations by adding an instruction such as the following:

* If you said that you were "dissatisfied" or "very dissatisfied".
  list those features of the course which caused this dissatisfaction.

  ....

  ....

A variation on the type of question illustrated above is to ask students to indicate the intensity with which they hold a viewpoint by responding on a scale which may vary in length from two points up to about ten. A simple example of a two-point scale is YES/NO and of a three-point scale is MORE/THE SAME/LESS. A decision whether to have an odd or an even number of choices is made on the basis of whether or not there is a clear mid-point to the scale, such as in the latter case above when students are asked whether the amount of work should be increased, decreased or remain the same. A scale with an even number of points is thought to be preferable when the evaluator wishes to polarise respondents' judgments as, for example, when the question asks students to rate the quality of a textbook. The responses can then be given a numerical value so that they may be more easily tabulated. Some caution should be exercised, however, in converting numerical values thus obtained into arithmetic means, as the pre-conditions (in parametric statistics) which apply to the calculation of a mean (or a standard deviation) have not been met. It is more honest to report the results in terms of the numbers (or percentages) of students responding to each category.

7.6. TYPES OF JUDGMENTS

An important feature of TenBrink's (1974) theoretical framework for the evaluation of teaching is the importance he places on the need for evaluation procedures which will provide adequate data so that informed judgments can be made about the quality of teaching and whether any changes should be made. There is little point in collecting data which cannot be used when making judgments or decisions. TenBrink's arguments apply equally to the evaluation of university courses. From the foregoing sections of this chapter it will be seen that data collected in surveys may be either quantitative or qualitative. It should be stressed that neither is more valid than the other; both contribute to the total picture.

7.6.1. Quantitative Data

Under this heading may be included such information as changes in student performance (bearing in mind the caveats expressed in the section on "Measures of Student Achievement"), response frequencies for multiple-choice questions and, what is more interesting, an analysis of how identifiable groups of students (e.g. mature age versus younger) respond to certain items in the questionnaire. Where open-ended questions have been used and the answers can be categorised, the frequencies of each type of response can also be expressed in quantitative terms.

7.6.2. Qualitative Data

In this category are included summaries of respondents' opinions and informed judgments of professional evaluators or other academics in the same field. Where the "professional evaluator" is the same person as the one writing the final evaluation report (as is likely to happen when a higher education unit is asked to conduct an evaluation) there is a danger that the views of the "professional evaluator" will unduly influence the tone of the final report. It is therefore desirable to have at least two people collaborating on each evaluation in order to ensure that the opinions of the one who observed classes are not given undue weight.

7.7. DECISIONS TO BE MADE

7.7.1. Changes in Content

Before any course evaluation is begun it is important to identify those areas where decisions are possible and changes can be made, and those over which the teacher has no control. There is little point, for example, in seeking student views on course content if that content is decided by some organisation outside the university such as a professional body (e.g. the Society of Engineers) or the State. If students want changes in content in this type of course, they need to lobby for support from students in equivalent courses in other institutions and also from people already working in the profession.

There are, however, many occasions when details of content are under the control of the person who teaches the course or the department or faculty in which the course is taught. In such cases student views should be sought on recommended deletions, additions and reorganisations. I would stress, however, that in the Australian scene at least, and probably in most countries where this book will be read, the final decision about course content will not be made by the students. After all, it is the university or college which awards the degree on the basis of judgments made by the faculty.

7.7.2. Changes in Teaching

As with content, there are certain decisions which are beyond the province of students, or even teachers. A recommendation to replace all lectures with small group seminars or discussions clearly has quite large financial implications as would a recommendation to increase the range or amount of laboratory work or introduce computer assisted learning. Nevertheless there are some changes which can be made to teaching methods without straining the budget. These include a limited change in balance between lectures, discussions, practical work and reading; a shift from a subject-centred to a problem-centred approach in teaching and learning; replacement of the textbook or reference material, and changing the patterns of assessment.

7.8. TARGET AUDIENCES FOR EVALUATION REPORTS

A course evaluation is primarily designed to identify strengths and weaknesses in a course and to suggest possible changes in content, organisation, teaching or assessment. The person for whom an evaluation report is most needed is therefore the teacher(s) in charge of the course. Other interested parties would be teachers in the same department, present and potential students, dean of the faculty, head of the department, and even professional bodies or potential employers. Despite the legitimate interest that each of the above groups may have, it is important to consider the implications of making the evaluation report available to people other than the teacher(s) most concerned. The reason for recommending against a wider dissemination of the report is that in a climate of university autonomy there is a danger that the teacher in charge will resist changes that are imposed by another person or group.

Evaluation reports only recommend changes; they have no legal power and should not even be seen to be coercive. This is even more important when those conducting the evaluation are also responsible for the improvement of teaching. Difficulties inherent in being both an evaluator and a helper are well documented. For example, Mulford (1985) refers to the "assess/assist dilemma" faced by school inspectors and classroom teachers. While recognising the desirability of making an evaluation report available only to the teacher(s) responsible for the course, an external evaluator might encourage the teachers themselves to distribute copies of the report to other interested parties, one argument being that a wider dissemination will demonstrate to others the teacher's willingness to evaluate the course and a commitment to improving it.

In keeping with the philosophy that course evaluations are primarily for the teachers of the course, it is wise to reject requests from deans or departmental review committees for course evaluations unless that request is supported by the teacher concerned. If, on the other hand, the course co-ordinator requests an evaluation of a course as part of a formal review, the questions asked would deal with matters most likely to be of interest to the review committee, such as the place of a particular course within the general program of a faculty or school and the extent to which this course prepares students for work in more advanced units.

7.9. SOME CONCLUDING THOUGHTS

This book began with a series of questions which a university or college teacher might ask about his or her own courses and teaching. In this final chapter we have examined some features of course evaluations. In conclusion it may be helpful for the reader to re-examine the original questions in the light of knowledge gained from earlier chapters in the book. The questions were:

- Why is this course being taught?

- What new knowledge, skills or attitudes do I expect my students to develop during this course?

- What levels of knowledge or skills do I expect in students when they enrol in this course?

- For students to develop the attributes listed above, what experiences do I need to provide for them during this course?

- Assuming equivalent backgounds on entry, will all students benefit from essentially the same experiences in the course?

- If students need to be offered a range of experiences. what variation is possible, given restraints on resources?

- What resources are available for teaching this course?

- Given the purposes of this course and the type of subject matter being learned, is there a logical order for the treatment of topics?

- How will I know whether this course is progressing satisfactorily?

- How will I know whether this course has been successful and whether certain changes would improve it for future groups of students?

REFERENCES

Abercrombie M.L.J. (1979) *Aims and Techniques of Group Teaching*
4th Ed.   Guildford   Society for Research into Higher Education

Aston, University of (1977) *Undergraduate Prospectus*
Birmingham   University of Aston

Ausubel D.P. (1963) *The Psychology of Meaningful Verbal Learning*
New York   Grune and Stanton

Ausubel D.P. (1967) "A cognitive-structure theory of school learning"
Chapter 8 in Siegel (1967)

Ausubel D.P., Novak J.D. and Hanesian H. (1978)
Educational Psychology A Cognitive View   2nd Ed.
New York   Holt, Rinehart and Winston

Baldwin T.S. (1971) "Evaluation of Learning in Industrial Education"
Chapter 22 in Bloom, Hastings and Madaus (1971)

Bassey M. (1981) "Pedagogic research: on the relative merits
of search for generalisations and study of single events"
Oxford Review of Education   7   pp. 73-94

Beard R.M. (1976) *Teaching and Learning in Higher Education*
Harmondsworth   Penguin (3rd Edition)

Beard R.M., Healey F.G. and Holloway P.J. (1974)
Objectives in Higher Education   2nd Ed.
London   Society for Research into Higher Education

Bligh D. (1972) *What's the Use of Lectures?*
Harmondsworth   Penguin

Bligh D. (1982) *Professionalism and Flexibility for Learning*
Guildford   Society for Research into Higher Education

Blishen E. (1969) *Blond's Encyclopaedia of Education*
London   Blond International

Bloom B.S. (ed.) (1956) *Taxonomy of Educational Objectives*:
*The Classification of Educational Goals. Handbook 1 -
Cognitive Domain*   New York   David Mackay

Bloom B.S., Hastings J.J. and Madaus G.F. (1971) *Handbook on
Formative and Summative Evaluation of Student Learning*
New York   McGraw-Hill

Boud D. (ed.) (1981) *Developing Student Autonomy in Learning*
London   Kogan Page   New York   Nichols

Braskamp L.A. (1980) "The role of evaluation in faculty
development" *Studies in Higher Education*   5:1   pp. 45-54

Brewer I.M. (1977) "SIMIG: A case study of an innovative
method of teaching and learning"
Studies in Higher Education 2:1 pp. 33-54

Britton J. *et al.* (1970) "Multiple marking of English compositions"
Chapter in *Schools Council Examinations Bulletin*, 12.

Brook R.J. and Thomson P.J. (1982)
"The evolution of a Keller Plan service statistics course"
Programmed Learning and Educational Technology 19:2, pp. 135-138

Centra J.A. (1979) *Determining Faculty Effectiveness*
San Francisco   Jossey Bass

Clift J.C. and Imrie B.W. (1981) *Assessing Students*:
Appraising Teaching   London   Croom Helm

Cockburn B. and Ross A. (1977a) *Lecturecraft*
Teaching in Higher Education Series: 1   Lancaster   School of Education

Cockburn B. and Ross A. (1977b) *Why Lecture?*
Teaching in Higher Education Series: 2   Lancaster   School of Education

Cockburn B. and Ross A. (1977c) *Working Together*
Teaching in Higher Education Series: 3   Lancaster   School of Education

Cockburn B. and Ross A. (1977d) *Participatory Discussion*
Teaching in Higher Education Series: 4   Lancaster   School of Education

Cockburn B. and Ross A. (1977e) *A Kind of Learning*
Teaching in Higher Education Series: 5   Lancaster   School of Education

Cockburn B. and Ross A. (1977f) *Patterns and Procedures*
Teaching in Higher Education Series: 6   Lancaster   School of Education

Cockburn B. and Ross A. (1977g) *Inside Assessment*
Teaching in Higher Education Series: 7   Lancaster   School of Education

Cockburn B. and Ross A. (1977h) *Essays*
Teaching in Higher Education Series: 8   Lancaster   School of Education

Cockburn B. and Ross A. (1977i) *The Use of Objective Tests*
Teaching in Higher Education Series: 9   Lancaster   School of Education

Collier K.G. (1984) "Higher education as preparation
for the handling of controversial issues"
Studies in Higher Education 9:1 pp. 27-35

Daniel J. (1975) "Learning styles and strategies:
the work of Gordon Pask" in Entwistle and Hounsell (1975)

Daniel J. (1983) "Independence and interaction in
distance education: New technologies for home study"
Programmed Learning and Educational Technology 20:3 pp. 155-160

Davies I.K. (1976) *Objectives in Curriculum Design*
Maidenhead   McGraw Hill

Dawes K. (1972)   "Behavioural objectives in science teaching"
Chapter 6.6 in Simpkins and Miller (1972)

Doyle K.O. (1983)   *Evaluating Teaching*
Lexington, Mass.   D.C. Heath and Company

Doyle K.O. and Crichton L.I. (1978)   "Student, peer and
self evaluations of college instructors"
Journal of Educational Psychology 70:5   pp. 815-826

Dressel P.C. and Marcus D. (1982) *On Teaching and Learning
in College*   San Francisco   Jossey-Bass

Dufresne R. (1978)   *Système d'Évaluation des Cours - Guide
d'Utilisation de la Banque d'Items* Québec   Université Laval SPU

Dunn S. (1967)   *Measurement and Evaluation in the Secondary
School* Melbourne   Australian Council for Educational Research

Dunstan M. (1959)   "The reliability of examiners in marking a
Leaving Certificate English examination"
Australian Journal of Education   3:3

Eble K.E. (1970)   *The Recognition and Evaluation of Teaching*
Washington, D.C.   The American Association of University Professors

Educational Testing Service (1963)   *Multiple-Choice Questions*:
A Close Look   Princeton, N.J.   E.T.S.

Engel C.E. and Clarke R.M. (1979)   "Medical education with a difference"
Programmed Learning and Educational Technology 16:1, pp. 70-87

Engel C.E., Clarke R.M. and Feletti G.I. (1982)   "The evolution
and impact of program evaluation in a new medical school"
Assessment and Evaluation in Higher Education 7:3, pp. 257-267

Entwistle N. (1981)   *Styles of Learning and Teaching*
Chichester   John Wiley

Entwistle N. (1982)   "Approaches and styles: recent research on
students' learning" *Educational Analysis* 4:2. pp. 43-54

Entwistle N. and Hounsell D. (eds) (1975)   *How Students Learn*
University of Lancaster

Eraut M. (1975)   "Should curriculum decisions be made 'for' or
'by' the independent learner?" in Furniss and Parsonage (1975)

Eraut M., Mackenzie N. and Papps I. (1975)   "The mythology of
educational development: reflections on a three-year study of
economics teaching."
British Journal of Educational Technology   6:3   pp. 20-34

Feletti G.I. (1980) "Evaluation of a comprehensive programme for the assessment of medical students" *Higher Education* 9, pp. 169-178

Feletti G.I., Saunders N.A. and Smith, A.J. (1983) "Comprehensive Assessment of Final-Year Medical Student Performance Based on Undergraduate Programme Objectives" *The Lancet* July 2 pp. 34-37

Ferguson G.A. (1966) *Statistical Analysis in Psychology and Education* (2nd Ed.) New York McGraw-Hill

Flood Page C. (1974) *Student Evaluation of Teaching: the American Experience* Guildford Society for Research into Higher Education

Furniss B. and Parsonage J.R. (eds) (1975) *Independent Learning in Tertiary Science Education* London Chemical Society Education Division

Gage N.L. (ed.) (1963) *Handbook of Research on Teaching* Chicago Rand McNally

Gagné R.M. (1965) *The Conditions of Learning* New York Holt, Rinehart and Winston

Gagné R.M. (1967) "Instruction and the conditions of learning" Chapter 10 in Siegel (1967)

Gagné R.M. (1971) "Learning theory, educational media, and individualized instruction" in Hooper (1971)

Gagné R.M. (1975) *Essentials of Learning and Instruction* Hinsdale The Doyden Press

Gibbs G. (1981) *Teaching Students to Learn: a Student-Centred Approach* Milton Keynes Open University Press

Gibbs G. (1982) *Twenty Terrible Reasons for Lecturing* Preston Standing Conference on Educational Development Services in Polytechnics (SCEDSIP)

Gibbs G. and Haigh M. (1983) *Alternative Models of Course Evaluation* Preston Standing Conference on Educational Development Services in Polytechnics (SCEDSIP)

Gosschalk F. *et al.* (1966) *Measurement of Writing Ability* New York College Entrance Examination Board

Graetzer H.G. (1972) "Cumulative experiments in the advanced laboratory" *American Journal of Physics* 40, pp. 270-276 (quoted in Ogborn, 1977)

Harman G.S., Miller A.H., Bennett D.J. and Anderson, B.I. (eds) *Academia Becalmed: Australian Tertiary Education in the Aftermath of Expansion* Canberra Australian National University Press

Hartog A.J. and Rhodes E.C. (1935) *An Examination of Examinations*
London   Macmillan

Heim A. (1976) *Teaching and Learning in Higher Education*
Windsor   NFER Publishing Company

Hooper R. (ed.) (1971) *The Curriculum: Context, Design and Development*
Edinburgh   Oliver and Boyd

Hooper R. (1983) "The computer as a medium for distance education"
Chapter 9 in Megarry *et al.* (1983)

Hounsell D. (1979) "Learning to learn: research and development
in student learning" *Higher Education* 8   pp. 453-469

Hounsell D. (1984) "Understanding teaching and teaching for understanding"
Chapter 11 in Marton, Hounsell and Entwistle,(1984)

Howe J. (1983) "Towards a pupil-centred classroom"
Chapter 6 in Megarry *et al.* (1983)

Hoyle E. (1983) "Computers and education: a solution in search
of a problem?"   Chapter 5 in Megarry *et al.* (1983)

Imrie B.W. (1983) "Specifications of a grading system"
Higher Education Research and Development   2:2   pp. 183-196

Isaacs G. and Imrie B.W. (1981) "A case for professional judgment
when combining marks" *Assessment and Evaluation in Higher
Education* 6:1 pp. 3-25

Johnstone A.H., Percival F. and Reid N. (1981) "Is knowledge enough?"
Studies in Higher Education 6:1, pp. 77-84

Kay S.M., O'Connell S. and Cryer P. (1981) "Higher levels of aims
in a physics laboratory: a first-year course at Royal Holloway College"
Studies in Higher Education   6:2   pp. 177-184

Keller F. (1968) "Goodbye, teacher"
Journal of Applied Behaviour Analysis 1. pp. 79-89

Keller F. and Sherman J.G. (1974) *The Keller Plan Handbook*
Reading, Mass.   W.A. Benjamin

Khan S.B. and Weiss J. (1973) "The teaching of affective responses"
Chapter 24 in R.M.W. Travers (ed.) *Second Handbook of Research
on Teaching*   Chicago   Rand McNally

Kiesler S., Siegel J. and McGuire T.W. (1984)   "Social Psychological
Aspects of Computer-Mediated Communication"
American Psychologist   39:10   pp. 1123-1134

Krathwohl D.R., Bloom B.S. and Masia B.B. (1964)
*Taxonomy of Educational Objectives: The Classification of
Educational Goals Handbook 2 Affective Domain*   New York   McKay

Lacey C. and Lawton D. (1981) *Issues in Evaluation and Assessment*
London   Methuen

Lamy T. and Henri F. (1983)   "Télé-Université: ten years of
distance education in Quebec" *Programmed Learning and
Educational Technology* 20:3   pp. 197-201

Laurillard D. (1979) "The processes of student learning"
Higher Education 8:4, pp. 395-409

MacDonald-Ross M. (1973)   "Behavioural objectives - a critical review"
Instructional Science 2, pp. 1-52

Maddison D. (1980)   "A medical school for the future: the Newcastle
experiment" *World Health Forum* 1:1-2, pp. 133-138

Mager R.F. (1962) *Preparing Objectives for Programmed Instruction*
San Francisco   Fearon

Marton F., Hounsell D. and Entwistle N. (1984)
The Experience of Learning Edinburgh   Scottish Academic Press

Marton F. and Säljö R. (1976)   "On qualitative differences in
learning. I - Outcome and process"
British Journal of Educational Psychology 46, pp. 4-11

McCormick R. (ed.) (1982) *Calling Education to Account*
London   Heinemann

McKeachie W.J. (1963)   "Research on teaching at the college and
university level" in Gage (1963)

McKeachie W.J. (1969) *Teaching Tips: a guidebook for the
beginning college teacher* Lexington   D.C. Heath and Company

Megarry J., Walker D.R.F., Nisbet S. and Hoyle E. (eds) (1983)
World Yearbook of Education 1982/83: *Computers and Education*
London   Kogan Page   New York   Nichols

Mehrens W.A. and Lehmann I.J. (1973) *Measurement and Evaluation
in Education and Society* New York   Holt, Reinhart and Winston

Miller A.H. (1980)   "First year programs in higher education"
Chapter 5 in Harman *et al.* (1980)

Miller A.H. (1984)   "The evaluation of university courses"
Studies in Higher Education 9:1   pp. 1-15

Miller C.M.L. and Parlett M. (1974)
Up to the Mark: A Study of the Examination Game
London   Society for Research into Higher Education

Moore M.R. (1967) *A Proposed Taxonomy of the Perceptual Domain and
Some Suggested Applications* Princeton   Educational Testing Service
cited in Bloom, Hastings and Madaus (1971)

Mulford B. (1984)   "On Teaching Educational Administration"
The Journal of Educational Administration   22:2   pp. 223-246

Myers I.B. (1962)   *The Myers-Biggs Type Indicator*: *Manual*
Princeton   Educational Testing Service

Nisbet J.D. and Entwistle N.J. (1970)   *Educational Reseach
Methods*   London   Hodder and Stoughton

Nuffield Foundation Group for Research and Innovation in
Higher Education (1976)   *Breadth and Depth: A Study of Curricula*
London   Nuffield Foundation

O'Connell S., Penton S.J. and Boud D.J. (1974)
A Rationally Designed Self-Service Laboratory Minicourse
University of Sussex Institute for Educational Technology

Ogborn J. (1977)   *Practical Work in Undergraduate Science*
London   Heinemann Educational Books

Parlett M. and Hamilton D. (1972)   *Evaluation as Illumination:
A New Approach to the Study of Innovatory Programmes*
Centre for Research in the Educational Sciences
University of Edinburgh   Occasional Paper No. 9

Pask G. (1972)   "A fresh look at cognition and the individual"
International Journal of Man-Machine Studies 4, pp. 211-216

Pask G. (1976)   "Styles and strategies of learning"
British Journal of Educational Psychology 46, pp. 128-148

Pask G. and Scott B.C.E. (1972)   "Learning strategies and individual
competence"   *International Journal of Man-Machine Studies*
4. pp. 217-253

Peck R.F. and Tucker J.A. (1973)   "Research on teacher education"
Chapter 30 in Travers (1973)

Perry W.G. (1970) *Forms of Intellectual and Ethical Development
in the College Years* New York   Holt, Rinehart and Wilson

Postlethwait S.N., Novak J. and Murray H. (1969)   *The Audio-Tutorial
Approach to Learning* 2nd Ed.   New York   Burgess

Prosser M.T. and Thorley N.T. (1981)   "Towards student self-direction
in first year undergraduate physics courses"
European Journal of Science Education 3, pp. 413-421

Ramsden P. (1979)   "Student learning and perceptions in the academic
environment"   *Higher Education* 8, pp. 411-427

Ramsden P. (1982)   "How academic departments influence
students' learning"   *HERDSA News*   4:3, pp. 3-5

Ramsden P. (1985) "Student learning research: retrospect and prospect"
Higher Education Research and Development   4:1,   pp. 51-69

Ramsden P. and Entwistle N. (1981)   "Effects of academic departments
in students' approaches to studying"
British Journal of Educational Psychology 51:3,   pp. 368-383

Roe E. and McDonald R. (1983)   *Informed Professional Judgment*:
a guide to evaluation in post-secondary education
Brisbane   University of Queensland Press

Rolph P. and Rolph J. (1982)   "A personal construct approach to
evaluating teaching practice"
Assessment and Evaluation in Higher Education   7:1, pp. 41-52

Rowntree D. (1974)   *Educational Technology in Curriculum*
Development   London   Harper Row

Rudduck J. (1978)   *Learning Through Small Group Discussion*
Guildford   Society for Research into Higher Education

Säljö R. (1982)   *Learning and Understanding*
Gothenburg   ACTA Universitatis Gothoburgensis

Satterly D. (1981)   *Assessment in Schools*   Oxford   Blackwell

Saunders N.A., Engel C.E. and Feletti G.I. (1982)
"Clinical supervisor's report"   *Medical Teacher*   4:4, pp. 151-154

Scanlon E. *et al.* (1982)   "Computer Assisted Learning"
Institutional Research Review   1, pp. 59-79

Shonle J.I. (1970)   "A progress report on open-ended laboratories"
American Journal of Physics   38, pp. 450-456 (quoted in Ogborn, 1977)

Siegel L. (ed.) (1967)   *Instruction: Some Contemporary Viewpoints*
San Francisco   Chandler

Simpkins W.S. and Miller A.H. (1972) *Changing Education*:
Australian Viewpoints   Sydney   McGraw Hill

Simpson E.J. (1966)   "The classification of educational objectives,
psychomotor domain"   *Illinois Teacher of Home Economics* 10
pp. 110-144   cited in Bloom, Hastings and Madaus (1971)

Smith A.B. (1977)   "Improving university teaching through the
identification of student-teacher learning styles"   in
The Use and Effects of Technological Advances for the Delivery
of Higher Education   Report on the Conference on Improving
University Teaching   Newcastle-upon-Tyne   pp. 272-280

Stirling, University of (1983)   *Prospectus for* 1984-85   Stirling

Stones E. (1981)   "Programmed learning revisited: a case study"
Programmed Learning and Educational Technology   18:1.   pp. 7-10

Taba H. (1962) *Curriculum Development: Theory and Practice*
New York   Harcourt, Brace and World

Tarrant R. (1982) "Programmed materials in business studies - diagnostic analysis for topic selection, program design, use and effectiveness"
Programmed Learning and Educational Technology 19:2 pp. 139-147

TenBrink T.D. (1974) *Evaluation: A practical guide for teachers*
New York   McGraw-Hill

Travers R.M.W. (ed.) (1973) *Second Handbook of Research on Teaching*
Chicago   Rand McNally

Trent J.W. and Cohen A.M. (1973) "Research on teaching in higher education" Chapter 32 in Travers (1973)

Tuckman B.W. (1975) *Measuring Educational Outcomes:*
Fundamentals of Testing   New York   Harcourt Brace

Tyler R.W. (1950) *Basic Principles of Curriculum and Instruction*
Chicago   University of Chicago Press

UTMU (University Teaching Methods Unit) (1976) *Improving Teaching in Higher Education*   London   University of London Teaching Methods Unit

Valette R.M. (1967) *Modern Language Testing: a handbook*
New York   Harcourt, Brace and World

Vaughan K. (1982) "University first year general chemistry by the Keller Plan (PSI") *Programmed Learning and Educational Technology* 19:2, pp. 125-134

Verma G.K. and Beard R.M. (1981) *What is Educational Research?*
Aldershot   Gower

Wieneke C. (1981) "The first lecture: implications for students who are new to the university" *Studies in Higher Education* 6:1, pp. 85-89

Woods D.R. (1983) "Introducing explicit training in problem solving into our courses" *Higher Education Research and Development* 2:1 pp. 79-102

Index